FINDING UNCONDITIONAL LOVE

A Little *Peace* at A Time

Experience the divine joy of spiritual freedom

JEANNE SANNER

Final Update - 2025

Finding Unconditional Love a Little Peace at a Time

By Jeanne Sanner

Jeanne's Unconditional Love Publishing, LLC

Information about the cover picture:
Photo used for the cover*
    Description
        English: Victoria Park, Kitchener, Ontario, Canada
        Date: 8 October 2012, 09:49:50
        Source: Own Work
        Author: Themightyquill (took the picture)
      *Picture has been modified with the image of the windblown dandelion

Printed in the United States of America

ISBN:
Paperback: 978-1-969367-27-4
Hardback: 978-1-969367-28-1
eBook: 978-1-969367-29-8

For permission requests, visit and write to the publisher at:
Jeanne's Unconditional Love Publishing, LLC
Go to **jeannesanner.love** and click on **Contact Me.**

KIRKUS
REVIEWS

TITLE INFORMATION

FINDING UNCONDITIONAL LOVE
A Little "Peace" at a Time
Jeanne M. Sanner
Okir Publishing Inc. (286 pp.)
$29.99 hardcover
ISBN: 978-1-4653-8009-8; May 16, 2018

BOOK REVIEW

An anecdotal account chronicles a spiritual journey to finding well-being.

The latest book from Sanner (*The Spirit of Unconditional Love*, 2008) charts a quest in life to realize the concept of unconditional love, which she defines with simple elegance: "*Thought that is without condemnation, founded on faith that is without doubt, fueled by emotion that is without fear, fused with kindness that is without boundary.*" The author characterizes this search as a voyage and her own self as a vessel heading to the destination of unconditional love. She extends the metaphor to the idea of barnacles encrusting the hull of that ship. She cautions her readers against a wide variety of barnacles, including ones that are attractive: "Some even seem appealing, and some I may even want to hang on to and show off, forgetting how destructive they really are." These barnacles can take many forms, each illustrated by Sanner in a series of stories and personal anecdotes: unhealthy twistings of thoughts, beliefs, and assumptions, which can be countered by seeking spiritual truths. "All things work for my spiritual well-being," Sanner writes, "when I choose to discover, digest and savor the nugget of unconditional love that is securely nestled in the nucleus of every event in my life." This openness to blessing runs throughout the book; readers are consistently reminded that the spiritual odyssey is not linear, vertical, or horizontal—or even external or internal—but rather a process of revelation. The author skillfully fleshes out these observations with tales from her own life, not only concerning her education, but also some of the triumphs and tragedies of her relationships. Her book encourages readers to engage in similar reflection, including sections for writing down their thoughts at the end of most chapters. Some of the guide's sentiments are vague to the point of being soppy ("Unconditional love is the only thing that can heal us when we think we need healing"). But readers on similar spiritual quests should find Sanner's account of her own expedition captivating.

An intriguing and broad-minded manual for spiritual enrichment.

Kirkus Indie, Kirkus Media LLC, 6411 Burleson Rd., Austin, TX 78744
indie@kirkusreviews.com

Praise

for

Finding Unconditional Love a Little Peace *at a Time*

For those not familiar with the book industry, Kirkus Reviews are highly respected. The reviewers are carefully selected to review books written within the genre and domain with which they have expertise, and they maintain very high standards for the works they review.

Sanner has received a highly positive Kirkus review for this book, and she has received wonderful reviews on Amazon.com.

She is encouraging everyone who reads her book to write a review on Amazon.com. She wants to hear the pros and cons of her book so she can improve upon her literary contributions in the future and to discover if her work is of value to you.

Dedication

To Laura Flynn: God's greatest earthly gift to me

And

To all those who seek, ask, and knock:
May this book be a positive stepping-stone on your
spiritual path.

Contents

Foreword

Dr. Linda McNamar

Many people live with remorse or guilt from incidents in their past which inhibits their expression of unconditional love in the present moment. Dr. Jeanne Sanner uses her own life experiences from her childhood until the present moment to demonstrate the spiritual insights she gained from living through them. Through compassion and understanding for both herself, and others, she learned to transform anger, ego, and rejection into lessons learned. Now, from her current perspective she shares with us not only her insights but how we can gain insight into our own lives.

This book is easy to read, sometimes sad, sometimes humorous but always grounded in spiritual understanding. I highly recommend that you read through the book once, all the way without stopping, and then take each chapter and spend some time re-reading and absorbing the message inherent within it. Take the time then to write your own thoughts. Whether you agree or disagree this practice will open you to your own life and the lessons to learn from it. It is a book to be read over and over.

I say keep it by your bedside and renew your quest for spiritual understanding each evening as you prepare to sleep. What better way could there be to spend that time between waking moments than to be steeped in unconditional love.

Preface

The style of this book is a little strange; it is most closely aligned with what is called *Stream of Consciousness*, which moves from one idea to another, sometimes with a connection, and sometimes as an isolated thought. There are no "chapters" per se, just numbered vignettes.

I weave my way from events in my life to my thoughts about things, and though it may seem disconnected at times, each numbered item does contribute to the overall theme—unconditional love.

I have included blank lines along the way, titled **Your Thoughts,** to give you an opportunity to have a conversation with the book.

To be honest, down the line, I believe what you choose to write on those blank lines will become more important than anything I have written. I hope you take advantage of the chance to chat.

There are innumerable advantages to living a life of unconditional love.

My hope is that you will find the way to make unconditional love your top priority so you can reap all the rewards that will come your way when you do.

Introduction

Is peace really possible? Is having a consistently joyful life possible? Is freedom from emotional, psychological, spiritual, and even physical pain possible?

Is unconditional love a myth? Does it mean that we accept everything just as it is and become a doormat for the world to wipe its muddy feet on?

Is unconditional love possible? Is it worth striving to achieve? Is it real? Is it achievable? Does it solve problems? Can it really create peace and joy? Can unconditional love eliminate guilt, demolish fears, and teach us how to forgive?

Can we discover what is blocking the experience of unconditional love? Are there ways to discover unconditional love, understand it, live it, and, ultimately, *be* it?

1. If you desire to have more peace and joy in your life

2. If you want less fear

3. If you want to eliminate guilt

4. If you desire to forgive yourself and others but can't seem to do it

5. If you find love to be elusive or even impossible

   Then put unconditional love as your top priority, and all your ifs will be resolved!

Finding Unconditional Love a Little* Peace *at a Time takes you through my lifetime of challenges and successes as I was seeking, knocking, and asking. Experience the miracles I have had in finding peace, joy, freedom, and unconditional love - miracles that have overcome events that, at first, seemed to stand staunchly in my way to happiness. I found my way through the labyrinth of fear and guilt.

Take this journey with me and find your own personal pathway to peace.

#1 On the Precipice

He was a very nice person when I married him, and I imagine he still is. We divorced less than a year after we were married. I just couldn't live the lie, and that's why I put the gun to my head and pulled the trigger.

He didn't deserve this. He had been married before. He confided in me that he had married a lesbian without knowing it. I couldn't tell him he had made the same mistake again. How could I; I wasn't even sure of that myself. All I knew was, I could not live a lie; I did not love him romantically or physically. I had to be true to myself, and in the process, all I was doing was hurting everyone I loved and everyone who loved me. The guilt was too much to bear.

I had had my doubts before we got married, but everyone said it was just pre- marital jitters. Anyone who experiences pre-marital jitters should not get married. It is one thing to be a little apprehensive about the future, but there should be no doubts about with whom you wish to share that uncertain part of your life. I had doubts.

I married Brent because that was the thing to do next in my life. I was twenty- three and single; I had graduated from college, secured (or so I thought) the dream career of teaching high school, and was dating the future son-in-law of my mother's dreams. He was bright, a college graduate with a great job, and very handsome in his Air Force officer's uniform. Perfect, or so it seemed on the outside.

Inside, I found myself physically attracted to one of my students, an eighteen- year-old senior, female student! She was only four years younger than I, but age did not matter, my position of authority in her life could not be usurped by personal desires, and it wasn't. I knew that, but I did not know . . . *What was wrong with me?*

Needless to say, the gun did not go off. To this day, I don't know why. All I remember was the deafening silence after I squeezed the trigger, and then my hand shaking, and then me becoming scared to death that the gun would go off, and my putting it down so it wouldn't.

I didn't know much about guns; I just remember my father wrapping my Brother Bobby's BB rifle around a tree after Bobby shot me in the hand accidentally.

I had watched Brent put the pistol together and then take it apart and put one portion of the gun in one drawer, and the other in another drawer.

I didn't bother to try to put it away after my failed attempt at suicide; I was too shaken. When Brent came home, he asked me why the gun was out, and I made up some excuse about wanting to fire it in the back yard to see what it was like . . . the back yard of the home his parents had bought for us as a wedding present. Oh, had I forgotten to mention that Brent's family happened to be very wealthy? I told Brent, "I think it jammed," and he said, "Well, it's a good thing it didn't go off, they would have heard it all over the neighborhood." And I said, "Yes; it's a good thing it didn't go off."

It was shortly after that, that I announced I wanted a divorce. Of course, nobody understood. How could they, neither did I. But it was a must; that's all I knew. Well, not all; I knew a pang of all-consuming guilt.

I left Brent with $.76 in my pocket (yes, 76 cents), no job (I had taken the place of a teacher who was not expected to return, but . . .), and no place to live (I would not live with my parents), and I was determined to never take a penny from Brent. I never wanted anyone to think I had married him for his money; I had not married him for his money.

I loved him as a person, but I had come to know that I could never be in love with Brent.

#2 The Smile

There are as many paths to unconditional love as there are people; there are as many twists and turns on those paths as there are moments in eternity. Though it did not stop there, my path started in a tiny Methodist church in a tiny little town in Maryland.

I was four, sitting in the sand in the backyard of our home drawing a cross with three long-stemmed flowers twirling up around it; it was my favorite thing to draw. The cross was not menacing; it was not sad; it was not death. In the Sunday school I attended, Jesus' body never hung on the cross; the cross was "something he rose above." In my innocence or my wisdom, the cross was a happy thing.

I was drawing a cross with three long-stemmed flowers crawling up when I "felt" someone smiling at me. I scooted around in the sand expecting to see Mommy, but no one was there, just a beautiful soft, yellow, pulsing light. I squinted to see who was "in" there. I didn't see anybody, but I liked the light a lot; it was very happy.

Then suddenly I knew who it was. "Oh! You're Jesus, aren't you? You're in there aren't you? Do you want to play in the sand with me?" I showed him what I was drawing. I felt his smile.

As a child, I experienced the visitor as a beautiful yellow light and felt its strong, loving, living energy hovering near me. The rippling light was very happy and very calm. It loved me completely just as I was. It had no expectations of me. I did not have to do anything or stop doing anything; I did not have to perform or withdraw; I did not have to speak or be quiet; I did not have to come or go; I did not have to change any part of me or pretend anything in any way; *I was just right just as I was.*

The light's smile was kind and gentle. As it lingered with me for a while, I felt its thoughts, and I remember thinking that it seemed very wise and that I wanted to grow up to be just like it. With that thought, I felt it come closer to me and surround me, and I seemed to feel boundless, and weightless, and I felt something I would not have been able to express then, but it would be what the terms "eternal" and "infinite" and "invulnerable" mean to me now. And I remember feeling something very unusual; I felt completely safe.

He stayed for a little while and then slipped away. I grinned; "He must be going to play with some other children he loves."

I finished my picture and went inside. Mom was washing breakfast dishes. "Jesus is a very nice man, isn't he Mommy?" Without hesitation, she said, "Yes he is, Jeanne."

I did not know then how many other enlightened figures
bring love into our lives!

I did not grasp the level of significance of the visit when I was four years old, and so, as the years passed, the tiny grain of time I shared with the light slipped into the sandbox of childhood memories.

At four, I giggled in the light's glow, but the light soon became overshadowed by the eclipse of time and punishment, and I found myself engulfed in darkness.

I wondered how I would ever find the light again.

#3 The Strop

I have a dark brown birthmark on the lower part of my left buttock. When I was a baby, it covered my whole cheek. So, when dad beat me with the leather razor strop on my bare bottom, he always made sure to hit me on the right cheek; I guess he was afraid of causing physical damage if he bruised the birthmark.

The most haunting experience with the strop happened while I was lying in bed reading the story of David and Goliath in a bible storybook with big print and wonderful, colored pictures. Dad said, "lights out" in his military voice. He was in the army, fought in WWII, and had recently come back from Korea.

David was just about to go out into the field to face the giant, so I kept reading. A shadow crossed the page; I looked up; there was my Goliath with leather strop in hand, but I had no slingshot. I had to pull down my pajama bottoms and bend over. I had to pee, so I said, "I have to go to the bathroom." But, when I got there, I couldn't go. I returned, bent over, took my "licks" and cried myself to sleep.

I wondered why God punished me for reading his stories.
It was years later I realized; it was not God who punished
me; God never does.

#4 Smoking

When I was seven, my cousin Pam—who is like a sister to me—and I were caught smoking. We were doing a great imitation of all the adults in our lives—my mom and dad, Pam's mom and dad, grandmother, Uncle Leo—and I had welts for days. It was far from the first time; I think it was the last.

Dad quit smoking after that.

Your Thoughts:

#5 Time

Time is fascinating. In my twenties, I came to define time as merely a man-made measurement of change. I realized that, if there were no change, there would be no time.

I also came to see that time in the physical world is always linear, and is, of course, measured by the rotation of the earth around the sun.

However, time in the mental world is not linear at all. We have all experienced moments that seemed like an eternity and hours that seemed like minutes. Time in the mental world is measured by the degree of the intensity of our focus.

Time in the emotional world is not linear, nor is it dependent on focus. Some of us have been marinated in a tragic moment from childhood that seeps into too many hours of each day, and some of us have had fleeting moments of joy we wish would last forever. Time in the emotional world is measured by our attachments.

Time in the spiritual world is infinity and eternally tied up with the ribbon of a single moment—a moment called *the now*. Time in the spiritual world cannot be measured at all; eternity can only be experienced. We have all experienced spiritual timelessness and its timeless wisdom; oh, if we could but shutter ourselves into that awareness for more than just a blink.

In the temporal world, our spiritual lives are measured by our experiences in discovering, living, and being, the unconditional love we truly are.

I wish to live my life in the Eternal Now, for that is the time in which peace and joy and freedom and unconditional love abide. I am determined to get there.

But when I was a child, a troubled teen, a confused young adult, the **now** *was not always where I wanted to be.*

#6 The Enemy beneath the Surface of the Sea

Before sailors set sail, they must complete a multitude of tasks to ensure that the vessel is shipshape. One vital task is to make sure they have rid their vessel of one of its most ominous enemies. This enemy has been a sailor's nemesis from the moment the first raft was built. It is seemingly innocuous, yet it is an insidious cause of destruction. It is not an intentional predator, yet, if it goes unattended, it can sink a ship! What is this innocent, yet potentially diabolical, entity? Barnacles.

Barnacles are invertebrates; they have no spines. They are crustaceans, which are prickly and sharp to the touch. They come in different shapes and sizes and colors. They have overlapping plates that create different shapes; they range from the size of a dime to that of a quarter, and come in white, dirty pink, brownish, and greyish green.

As adults, they adhere to rocks, wood pilings, even animals such as whales, and of course, ships. They adhere themselves with a substance they produce that is one of the strongest natural epoxy-like types of cement known to man. In fact, their substance sticks to Teflon! And they stay adhered to that surface for the rest of their lives. There can be at least 100 barnacles per square foot of surface on a ship, including rudders and hulls. If they weren't so dangerous, they could be considered great topics for an interesting conversation.

Barnacles cost the shipping industry billions of dollars every year; they speed up corrosion, create drag resistance, reduce speed, interfere with maneuverability, and can sink boats. Millions of dollars are spent on research and development to find ways to release the adhesive and prevent barnacles from sticking to ships.

The focus has become "prevention."

Scraping barnacles off the surface is the most common way to rid ships of the problem, but scraping has not proven to be effective, and no one to date has developed a chemical to remove barnacles in a cost-efficient way.

Shipping companies have tried covering wooden-hulled ships with lead, copper, and other metals, all of which, of course, are costly and create other problems to solve. Recently, some have applied toxic paints to their vessels, but now evidence is demonstrating that those toxic paints are harming the environment.

There is an exploration into sharkskin. Barnacles do not adhere to sharks. So, companies are exploring ways to replicate sharkskin and cover their ships with that.

So, What Does this Have to Do with Unconditional Love?

I have a spiritual vessel, which appears vulnerable to the emotional and psychological barnacles floating through the sea of life that adhere to me in a very strong way. They are spineless, prickly, and sharp to the touch. They come in all shapes, sizes, and colors of the emotional spectrum. Some even seem appealing, and some, I may even want to hang on to and show off, forgetting how destructive they really are.

They adhere to the very ethereal sinews of my heart and mind, the very hulls and rudders of *my soul* I allow them to attach themselves to me, and they stick with such a strong epoxy-like cement it seems impossible to rid myself of them or to prevent them from clinging to me for the rest of my life. It seems so many of them can live on such a small surface of my spiritual vessel that I can become overwhelmed by them.

"Emotional" barnacles cost me thousands of hours in distress and pain when I could be experiencing peace and joy. They speed up the corrosion of my body and mind; they create drag resistance, slowing me down and pulling me under. They interfere with my maneuverability throughout my relationships, and they can sink my vessel into a deep mire of sorrow and despair.

I spend hundreds of hours and dollars on research and development with self-help books, counseling sessions, and medications, often to no avail. Some of the chemicals I try merely cover up the barnacles, hiding them rather than releasing them. Scraping creates damage and leaves scars.

I could attempt prevention by using defense mechanisms, but they are more of a diversion than a solution, so I stay raw and vulnerable.

What constitutes the epoxy-like glue that cements my psychological barnacles to *my soul*? How can I combat it? What is the nature of those barnacles? How do I release them? How do I prevent them from ever sticking to me again?

The answers are simple and complex; easy and difficult; obvious and obscure; accessible, doable, and freeing.

The "Solvent" is Unconditional Love.

The "Shield" is Faith.

> *But what is unconditional love, and what is faith, and where can I get them?*

#7 Einstein

Albert Einstein said,

A human being is part of a whole, called by us the "universe," a part limited in time and space. He experiences himself, his thoughts, and feelings, as something separated from the rest—a kind of optical delusion of his consciousness. This delusion is a kind of prison for us, restricting us to our personal desires and affection for a few persons nearest us. Our task must be to free ourselves from this prison by widening our circles of compassion to embrace all living creatures and the whole of nature in its beauty. [1]

#8 What Is Unconditional Love?

I have come to realize that my spiritual journey is not linear, or vertical, or horizontal, or external, or internal, or circular, or spiral. My spiritual journey does not move me in any direction; it simply unveils the truth of who I really am.

The question becomes, "Who am I, really?"

I have come to realize that I live in many different worlds concurrently, and I am a different "me" in each world. In the physical world, I am a body. In the mental world, I am the total accumulation of all my thoughts. In the emotional world, I am a reflection of the scope of my faith. In the spiritual world, I am an eternal thread of unconditional love woven together with others into a perfect spiritual fabric of oneness.

In my early teens, the conscious memory of the smile within the golden glow returned in all its innocence and glory, and I began to explore spirituality with a deep desire and great sincerity. Upon re-living my moment with the light, I gained a more mature insight into unconditional love. The memory showed me what unconditional love is and what it is not. I began to question whether I could love unconditionally and, despite the sense of safety the light gave me when I was four, I began to question whether I was worthy of being loved unconditionally. Is unconditional love merely an ideal, a wish, a dream, or is it something very much within my grasp?

My search has taken me on a journey packed with unexpected discoveries, the most important of which is that unconditional love is an experience, not a destination.

I experience unconditional love when I choose to see beyond the "veil." When I choose to have perceptions and beliefs that reach beyond the "conditions" of my current experience and discover the essence of the world—love—that lies beyond all conditions, that's when I experience unconditional love.

I experience unconditional love when I choose to see beyond "evil." When I choose to have perceptions and beliefs that are free from viewing myself as a victim and discover that the external world has only the amount of power over me that I grant it, that's when I experience unconditional love.

I experience unconditional love when I choose to "live"—to live free of fear. When I choose to have perceptions and beliefs marinated in the knowingness that ALL things work together for my spiritual well-being, and when I choose to seek the spiritual truths baked into each morsel of life, that's when I taste unconditional love.

When I choose to have perceptions and beliefs that see the spiritual truth about others and myself—that we are, at our very core, unconditional love itself—and when I am compelled to express that truth through boundless kindness, that's when I experience unconditional love as I clumsily stumble down the path to perfect peace.

Simply put, unconditional love is: *Thought that is without condemnation, founded on faith that is without doubt, fueled by emotion that is without fear, fused with kindness that is without boundary.*

Unconditional love has an unmistakable look. Unconditional love exudes peace, patience, understanding, kindness, gentleness, humility, strength, hope, faith, wisdom, compassion, eternity, infinity, oneness, and lots of joy!

Unconditional love has no doctrine. Unconditional love lifts people up, seeks only itself in all things, and creates everlasting peace and joy.

The pursuit of discovering, understanding, living, and coming to "be" unconditional love springs from the living river of truth that flows within each of us. We are all born with all spiritual knowledge; that knowledge often gets smothered in the quagmire of the physical world, but I can, and I will, find it and bring it to the surface of my consciousness.

Great examples of unconditional love, such as Abraham of the Old Testament, Siddhartha Gautama (Buddha), Jesus, Mohammad, Gandhi, Martin Luther King, Nelson Mandela, and so many more, convince me that unconditional love is indeed possible, and they have shown me ways to experience it.

One of the greatest examples of someone who chose unconditional love in the most trying of circumstances is Viktor Frankl, a Holocaust survivor who wrote *Man's Search for Meaning* in which he said:

> The one thing you can't take away from me is the way I choose to respond to what you do to me. The last of one's freedoms is to choose one's attitude in any given circumstance . . . Love is the only way to grasp another human being in the innermost core of his personality. No one can become fully aware of the essence of another human being unless he loves him. (2)

THE Spirit of Unconditional Love (**THE SOUL**) is known by different names throughout the world and throughout the history of humankind, and it speaks with everyone who seeks to converse. Each of us can experience being loved unconditionally and can experience loving others and ourselves unconditionally because unconditional love is our true essence. Each of us will achieve coming to the fullness of the unconditional love we are.

The question becomes . . . How?

Your Thoughts:

#9 Across the Ocean

Lassie died, and we went to Europe. Our collie, Lassie (of course) was my best friend. She became a member of our family shortly after I was born. I shared all my ideas with her, which she always understood no matter what language I spoke—baby talk, kid talk, silence, or hugs. I shared my toys, laughter, tears, joys, and my ice cream cones; we both loved vanilla best.

Dad had heard the screeching tires about a half mile away, and when she didn't come home at her usual time, we went looking. We lived in a rural town with lots of territories to cover. "Lassie, Lassie, come on, girl. It's time for dinner . . . Lassie . . ." Dad found her; she was lying peacefully in a field; she had been hit by a car and wandered into the field to die. I cried all the way to Germany.

Dad got stationed in Kaiserslautern. We took the ship the **Upshire**, which we called the "Upchuck." I won a watch at Bingo; the next day, as I leaned over the railing, it fell off my wrist and drifted to the depths of the sea.

*Luck is fickle. Attachments are painful. It was 1958, and
I was twelve.*

#10 Attachments

Quests often meet with obstacles, and the quest for unconditional love is no exception. If I want to change my life by experiencing more unconditional love, I need to find the answers to two questions: What are the obstacles I need to overcome, and how can I overcome them?

My personal search revealed that the "epoxy-like" glue adhering spiritual barnacles to my soul is comprised of three elements: attachments, fears, and condemnation. Attachments create fears; fears create condemnations; condemnations create separation; separation creates pain and suffering.

If I can find the solvent that dissolves these sticky substances in my life and find a shield to protect me from further incidents of clinging barnacles, then I will experience the unconditional love I seek.

I discovered that there are specific steps I can take to achieve my spiritual goal. The following parable demonstrates the first step toward creating that change in my life.

A Cup of Tea

> Nan-in, a Japanese Master during the Meiji era (1868-1912), received a university professor who came to inquire about Zen.
>
> Nan-in served tea. He poured his visitor's cup full, and then kept on pouring.
>
> The professor watched the overflow until he no longer could restrain himself. "It is overfull. No more will go in!"
>
> "Like this cup," Nan-in said, "you are full of your own opinions and speculations. How can I show you Zen unless you first empty your cup?"

I have discovered, I always think I am right. Obviously, I would not continue to think what I am thinking if I thought what I was thinking was wrong, so I always think I am right, and I think many people are like me.

My seeking for spiritual truth must begin with the realization that, just because I think I am right, does not mean that I am.

Seekers of truth begin their search by relinquishing their attachments to their current beliefs—even when, at the beginning of their search, they believe that they "know" the "truth" and that they know what is right. Consequently, my journey has led me to incorporate into my life ideas from many sources of spiritual insight. My search for truth produces its best results when I seek a boundless sea of insights. Part of my journey took me to Buddhism. It was there that I discovered something that brought me many miles closer to spiritual awareness, the realization that there is one huge obstacle in my way to reaching nirvana - *attachment*. That one insight has brought me much closer to a sense of constant peace. Relinquish my attachments, and I will be free to experience freedom, peace, joy, and unconditional love.

I also discovered that there are many things to which I have become attached. Following are eight difficult attachments / barnacles to release: (1) Fears (2) Guilt (3) Current beliefs (rules, *shoulds, should nots, musts, must nots,* prejudices) (4) Assumptions; (5) Expectations; (6) Control; (7) Need to be right, and (8) Ego.

Yikes! Where do I begin?

#11 The Man in the Attic

The irony about fear is that the more we focus on being safe, the more frightened we become. I grew up in a small town and a small home. There were only two bedrooms. As we got older, my brother, Bobby, needed his own room. My folks converted the attic.

I was about five. My parents had guests who were spending the night; a cot was set up in Bobby's room for me to sleep on while the guests used my room. It was the first night I had ever slept somewhere other than the bedroom I had always used.

The light was strangely different in the attic. The moonbeams came in and created scary shadows on the slanted ceiling and narrow walls, but I nestled into the clean sheets and blanket, closed my eyes, and was about to drift to sleep when something startled me.

I opened my eyes and saw a man sitting at the end of my bed rocking back and forth! He had a hat on, and he just sat there rocking back and forth. I froze! I stopped breathing. I didn't move a muscle! I knew, if I moved, he would discover me. I lay there praying that the sweat dripping down my face wouldn't make a sound; the more I tried to hold my breath, the more I needed to breathe, I was fighting not to cough, not to cry.

Then . . . my big toe jerked! It just jerked! I don't know why it jerked, but the big toe on my right foot jerked. I knew without a doubt that the man at the end of my bed had seen my big toe jerk under the blanket, and now he knew I was there! I didn't think; I just jumped out of bed, turned on the light, and swung my little body around to meet him face-to-face. I was looking right at "him"! "He" was Bobby's baseball cap hanging on the rocking chair that moved each time a car went by. I didn't laugh; I was too young to see the humor. I didn't cry; I knew I was safe, but I did learn a lot.

I learned that fears are merely illusions that disappear in the light.

#12 Barnacle 1: Fear

Fear is the largest cluster of barnacles I need to loosen from my soul. Fear of rejection, pain, retaliation, anguish, disappointment, and more; fear can, without a doubt, sink my ship!

When I taught Psychology, one homework assignment I gave the students was to make a list of at least fifteen emotions. (You may want to stop and make your own list.)

The next day, the students would make two columns on a piece of paper; one "positive" and one "negative," and re-write the emotions from their original list into the appropriate columns.

The students discovered two things: most listed more negative than positive emotions, and that there are really only two emotions from which all others stem.

Two Wolves

A Cherokee elder was teaching his grandchildren about life. He said to them, "A fight is going on inside of me. It is a terrible fight between two wolves.

One wolf is fear, anger, envy, hate, sorrow, regret, greed, arrogance, self-pity, guilt, resentment, inferiority, lies, pride, and superiority.

The other wolf is joy, peace, hope, love, sharing, serenity, humility, kindness, benevolence, friendship, empathy, generosity, truth, compassion, and faith.

This same fight is going on inside of you and every other person too."

The grandchildren thought about it for a minute and then one child asked, "Grandfather, which wolf will win?"

The old man simply replied . . . "The one I feed." [3]

I began to discover what I call, *Laws of Emotion*. The first law being: Love and Fear are the two primary emotions from which all other emotions stem. All negative emotions, including anger, hate, and prejudice stem from fear, and all positive emotions come from love.

When I became more aware in life that all my emotional pain and anger are a direct result of fear, it became easier for me to get a grip on my feelings; I merely needed to understand the fear that was causing the pain and begin to address that fear.

The core of fear is rooted in the sense of a loss. One important sense I had lost was the sense of feeling safe. Other times the core of my pain dealt with the fear of not having control, or the fear of being wrong, or the fear of disappointing people, or the fear that my desires and expectations would not be met, or the fear of losing a loved one or a friend, or the fear of losing the respect of others or losing respect for myself.

Then, I discovered the second *Law of Emotion*: Faith and Fear are mutually exclusive; whenever I am experiencing fear, I am lacking faith; if I have faith, I cannot experience fear.

The third *Law of Emotion* is: In the temporal world, there can be no peace without freedom; there can be no freedom without choice.

The choice is simple—love or fear. The choice is complex—love or fear.

#13 Trouble Brewing in Germany

I didn't have to be politically savvy to know trouble was brewing in Germany in 1958; planes breaking the sound barrier, mandatory evacuation drills—evacuations not of the building but of the country—and constant, intense energy in the air gave me all the clues I needed. Emergency clothes, papers, IDs, and phone numbers filled the bottom drawer of my dresser. I kept the list of evacuation essentials behind my picture of Jesus on the wall in my bedroom.

There were poodle skirts, crinolines, rock and roll, and borders, lots of borders. I don't remember much, just that Mom seemed worried. We were tourists attempting to enter East Berlin. There was no wall; not yet, that came in 1961, but there was a guarded checkpoint. Other tourists were waved beyond the gates, but we had been stopped.

Two hours later, Dad was still inside the building; we were still inside the car. I sensed danger; I didn't know why. Mom tried to keep us distracted, but her own fears were evident. It was years later that I began to understand why a US Army Warrant Officer would have been detained. We didn't get to tour East Germany; we were turned away; that was the first border incident, but it wasn't our last.

Your Thoughts:

#14 Barnacle 2: Beliefs

Muddy Road

Tanzan (`tan-zan) and Ekido (e-`key-doe) were once traveling together down a muddy road. Heavy rain was still falling.

Coming around a bend, they met a lovely girl in a silk kimono and sash, unable to cross the intersection.

"Come on, girl," said Tanzan at once. Lifting her in his arms, he carried her over the mud.

Ekido did not speak again until that night when they reached a lodging temple. Then he no longer could restrain himself. "We monks don't go near females," he told Tanzan, "especially not young and lovely ones. It is dangerous. Why did you do that?"

"I left the girl there," said Tanzan. "Are you still carrying her?" [4]

I love this parable. It speaks to so many of the most difficult attachments there are to release. "Muddy Road" brings to light the often-misguided power of beliefs, laws, and rules, and it beautifully highlights the choices available when there is a conflict between following the letter of the law and following the spirit of the law.

This parable demonstrates how choosing to follow the spirit of the law can bring about a more positive response and create a more positive consequence; often, the weight of rigidity can pull us into an unforeseeable pool of quicksand.

The two main characters of the Zen parable are monks. The monks are aware of the law, or expectation, that they are to avoid contact with beautiful young women because of the potential conflicts any interest in a woman might create for a monk.

This law, this belief, is a reasonable one. This moral boundary is not worthy of civil disobedience or blatant rebellion; the rule is one of common sense and wisdom.

However, wisdom does not have a narrow or rigid nature; it is as fluid as the circumstances in life.

Tanzan broke the letter of the law by first paying attention to the young woman in distress, and secondly by picking her up and carrying her across the muddy road. In the last sentence of the parable, Tanzan's response to Ekido's concerns indicates that Tanzan recognizes that he broke the letter of the law by carrying a distraught woman across the muddy road, but he also makes it clear that he put her down on the other side and left her there. He did not carry her in his heart or his mind thereafter. He did not dwell on her or have second thoughts.

Tanzan followed the spirit of the law by not becoming obsessed, disturbed, or distracted by the fact that he was helping a young lady. He merely assisted a fellow human being in need, which is also an expectation of a monk.

On the other hand, even though Ekido did not physically carry the young lady across the muddy road, she was in the clutches of his thoughts and his emotions for the rest of the day and into the night. Thus, Ekido, who was more distracted and disturbed by the young lady than Tanzan, followed the letter of the law, because his beliefs dictated that he should not pick the young lady up, but he broke the spirit of the law. If he had been alone and had followed the letter of the law without re-examining his beliefs, the young lady would have remained stranded by the road.

Thus, Tanzan, the monk who followed the spirit of the law, provided the greatest service with the least amount of personal conflict.

This parable reminds me how important it is to stop and examine my own beliefs and choices. Am I more like Ekido or Tanzan? Do I maintain unexamined beliefs, rules, and shoulds? Do I question the origin of the rule and its deepest intent? Do I always follow the letter of the law regardless of the consequences? Can I have the courage to break the letter of the law and follow the spirit of the law if I find them in conflict? Do I find myself getting frustrated with those who believe differently than I do?

What do I tend to dwell on about someone else's behavior? Am I expecting them to act a certain way? And when they don't, do I get stuck on the "shoulds"? How many "shoulds" do I put on myself? How many "shoulds" do I put on other people? Are they justified? Why? Why not? Am I judging the heart, mind, and soul of another person based on my own "shoulds"? Can I easily "render unto Caesar that which is Caesar's and unto God that which is God's"? What I am carrying around that I could simply put down on the side of the road?

My "shoulds" may drown me in the cesspool of my own
unloving values.

#15 France

Prejudice was a mystery to me. I had never experienced it; I was a WASP (White Anglo-Saxon Protestant) in a town buzzing with WASPS. Though I didn't know what that meant then, I did know that I had never felt the sting of hatred directed at me for no reason at all. We were going on a vacation; we wanted to tour France. The French hated us: Americans. Others had warned us. If the French guards at the border knew we were Americans, they would make things difficult.

The guards stopped us at the border. They inspected our car. Dad had cans of gasoline in the back of the station wagon; gas stations were few and far between; being stranded in a foreign country was scary. The guards decided to confiscate our gasoline; Dad refused; they insisted; Dad dumped the gasoline on the ground; they granted us entry into their beautiful country of green rolling hills and quaint towns.

Prejudice is still a mystery to me.

#16 Barnacle 3: Assumptions

The parable *Muddy Road* also addresses assumptions. Assumptions are conclusions people reach and believe are true based on limited, wrong, or popular pieces of information. Many people are familiar with a saying about the word assume that warns us of potential dangers. "When you assume, you make an "ass" of 'u' and 'me.'"

The saying is cute and clever; however, the problem is that assumptions are much more complex than that. We must make assumptions in order to maintain a semblance of sanity! We cannot avoid drawing conclusions about situations, people, and circumstances throughout the day. I assume my car will start; if it does not, I immediately begin to assume—the battery is dead, or the ignition is damaged, or I have run out of gas, or . . . I work from these assumptions to solve the problem.

In other words, it is often a good and necessary thing to make assumptions. Assumptions in and of themselves are not the problem; it is the types of assumptions we make that can create a problem. The following are three types of assumptions:

1. **Valid/justifiable**: These assumptions are based on multiple, personal past experiences. Someone comes in late—I assume it is Rose. The phone rings—I assume it is for me. The dog is

barking—I assume the mail person is at the door.

2. **Invalid/unjustifiable**: These assumptions are based on stereotypes. He's single, so he must be gay. She has tattoos, so she must be in a gang. He is only being kind to get attention. (The last example assumes you know the deepest motives someone has for his/her behavior, and that is a very dangerous assumption to make!)

3. **Logical/unsubstantiated**: These assumptions are based on weak logic. He looks Hispanic, so he probably doesn't speak English. She has a big belly, so she must be pregnant. She is wearing a headscarf, so she must be going through chemotherapy. These assumptions are logical, but if you ask the woman with the big belly when the baby is due and she is not pregnant, you may experience an uncomfortable moment!

Now that I know that assumptions are barnacles that can pull me away from unconditional love, I find it important to examine my assumptions carefully. Is my assumption valid/justifiable? Is my assumption loving and non-judgmental? What assumptions am I making about others and their intentions? That's what Ekido did to Tanzan. Ekido assumed that because Tanzan picked up the young lady, he could not "put her down." He was wrong. Do I do that to others? Do I do that to myself? If so, how can I change it?

Sometimes there can be lethal consequences when the barnacles of fear, belief, and assumption breed.

#17 Dachau: *Why?*

I don't know why they thought it would be a good idea for a twelve-year-old girl to see Dachau, a WWII Nazi concentration camp, but my parents took my brother and me there. I don't know how it affected Bobby; we never talked about it; he was fifteen then.

I saw the cement building where prisoners were told they would be taking a shower but were gassed to death instead. I saw "blood ditch" where prisoners were lined up, and shot, and where their bodies would fall on top of each other as they were thrust into the hole by the force of the bullets. I saw the ovens—they were so small, so narrow. "How could they fit people into these ovens?" Mom took me to see the pictures, and then I knew; there was nothing left of them; they were walking skeletons. I didn't understand. I sobbed. *Barnacles can be deadly.*

#18 What Unconditional Love Is Not: Part I

Unconditional love is not any part of condemnation, doubt, fear, needs, grievances, pain, vengefulness, attachment, or attack. Unconditional love is not foolish or blind. Unconditional love is not ignorant. Unconditional love is not stupid.

Unconditional love is seeing without condemnation and is steeped in wisdom.

How in the world do I get there from here?
How *in* the world do I get there from here?
How in *the* world do I get there from here?
How in the *world* do I get there from here?
How in the world *do* I get there from here?
How in the world do *I* get there from here?
How in the world do I *get* there from here?
How in the world do I get *there* from here?
How in the world do I get there *from* here?
How in the world do I get there from *here*?

#19 Paris: A Nightmare

The military forced Dad to retire early; his European tour was going to end after two years instead of three. Time was short. Mom and Dad wanted to see Paris on their own; they decided to go. They sat Bobby and me down in the living room to go over the plans. They were very matter-of-fact. "We don't think it will happen, but if you have to evacuate while we're gone, you are to leave with the family on the third floor."

"What do you mean, 'You don't *think* it will happen, but . . .'?" I didn't know the people on the third floor! Bobby did; he was friends with their son. "Why do you have to go to Paris? Why are you going if there's a chance it might happen—that we might have to leave Germany? How will we all get back together? Where will Bobby and I go? How will you find us? Don't go! Please don't go!"

They went.

The Dream

From left to right, we were side-by-side—Dad, Mom, Bobby, and me. We were in a cement room: the walls were cement; the floor was cement; everything was cement grey. We stood up against one wall; we faced another wall that had a trench dug in front of it. There was one small window high on the wall ahead of us letting grey, dim light spray across the room. Soldiers with rifles stood across from us against that wall with the ditch in front of them. Upon command, one soldier raised his rifle and fired a single bullet. It was a wooden bullet like the ones used in WWI. It hit me on my right side and took away part of my waist. Another soldier ran and retrieved the bullet and returned it to the rifleman. He fired again, just at me. Dad and Mom and Bobby stood there looking straight ahead. It hit the same place on my right side, and it tore away more of my waist; I bled. After the third bullet hit me, we were allowed to take a break.

Mom and I went to the ladies' room; Dad and Bobby went to the men's room. While mother was putting on lipstick, I kept asking, "Why are they only shooting at me? How can we get out of here? How can we escape?" Mother brushed her hair. We had to go back into the room. One rifleman fired again; this time he hit my left side; the soldier ran to retrieve the bullet, and I woke up.

Geometry

It happened in Geometry class while my parents were in Paris. I started screaming, yelling, and crying. I had never failed a test before. The teacher sent me out to the hall. I had never been sent out in the hall before. I got called out of History class to go to the counselor's office. I had never been called to the counselor's office.

What I remember telling the counselor was that I liked the stamp collection I started; I'm sure there had to be more. Did I talk about the things I was really screaming and yelling and crying about? Did I talk about the dream? Did I talk about abandonment? Did I talk about abuse? I must not have; I never had to go to the counselor's office again. I didn't understand anything that happened that day, not then; I do now.

#20 Antidotes to Fear

1. The antidote to my own fears lies in the knowledge of what I truly am.

2. The antidote to the fears I see in others lies in extending what I truly am to them.

What I truly am is unconditional love.

#21 Brussels: A Glimpse of Oneness

It was a wonderful experience, The Brussels World's Fair. We stayed in a private home of a family who had volunteered to take in total strangers who traveled to Brussels for the Fair. They had children my age who could speak five languages fluently; fortunately, they chose English when speaking to me (☺). They were warm, loving, caring people. I feel it now as I reflect on them.

Dad took a phenomenal picture of the Atomium, a permanent structure built specifically for the Brussels World's Fair. It represents an exploding atom. Each round ball is covered with lights, each blinking at a different time. It is nearly impossible to capture a picture at night of the rare moments when all the lights are on at the same time. Dad did it; it is spectacular, and so was that moment.

In the picture, with all the lights glowing together, the Atomium was one with itself; it was whole; it was at peace, and so was I for a moment.

#22 The Foundation of Faith

An exploding atom - there it was before us in Brussels, but do atoms really exist? Scientists debate whether we can capture the image of an actual atom through a special microscope, but even without the physical evidence, innumerable scientific theories are based on the "faith" that atoms exist.

When I taught Critical Thinking, I used to ask the students, "Do you have a mind? Not a brain, a mind. If yes, please raise your hand." All hands went up.

Then I would ask, "What color is your mind?" They didn't know. "How much does your mind weigh?" They didn't know. "What shape is your mind?" "What does it feel like to the touch?" "What does it smell like?" "Does it make any noise; if so, what kind?" "Where does it come from?" They didn't know.

How then do I prove I have a mind?

It is impossible to prove that I have a mind by using direct physical criteria as evidence; yet, I know I have a mind. The proof lies in my behavior. I move, I speak, I analyze, I calculate, I solve, I question, I write, I think. Even though these behaviors are not direct physical evidence of a mind, I accept them, through inductive reasoning, as proof that my mind exists. Faith is trust without doubt. I have faith that I have a mind.

When seeking evidence of spiritual truths, I must make the same concession. By the mere fact that I am seeking something spiritual, by definition, I have eliminated the possibility of finding direct physical evidence; otherwise, I would be seeking something physical, not something spiritual. However, I can, through inductive reasoning, conclude from physical, mental, and emotional events that the spiritual does exist.

I have experienced that spiritual evidence finds me when I seek it. When I choose to look through a spiritual lens, I see evidence of spiritual truths; when I look through the lens of my ego, I see evidence of worldly things. Finding unconditional love happens when I choose to look through a spiritual lens to gaze upon the things of the world.

When I took my first science class in high school, I learned how to use a microscope. It did not take me long to learn how it worked, and I quickly discovered that it is a powerful tool. When I used it properly, it opened my eyes to many truths about the world that I otherwise would not have been able to see or experience.

An important feature of the microscope is the knob that moved the tube that held the lens. Turning the knob adjusted the focus of the lens to suit my eyesight. Of course, the adjustment did not change anything on the slide that I was examining; in fact, it did just the opposite; the adjustment ensured I would see the contents of the slide clearly.

I was particularly grateful for that mechanism since the person with whom I shared the microscope had poor vision. When it came to my turn to examine a slide after she did, if I had had to keep the adjustment where she put it, I would have seen nothing but fuzzy images, and the same was true for her when using the microscope after I did.

A microscope is a valuable tool, and when used properly, it can reveal many truths about the physical world that would otherwise remain a mystery. I view the *Bible,* the *Koran,* the *Talmud,* the *Bhagavad-Gita,* the *Upanishads, A Course in Miracles,* other sacred writings, and individual experiences as microscopes designed to help me peer into the heart of unconditional love.

Just as in science class, I learned how to use the microscope in a short time and spent most of each class looking at slides, I believe that it is important to spend more time looking at the slides of life rather than debating over the nuts and bolts of the "microscopes."

Just as our physical vision differs from person-to-person, our spiritual vision varies as well. It is important for us to be able to see the slides of unconditional love, and our relationships, and our behaviors, and other elements of life clearly. Without fuzzy vision, we must adjust the microscopes to see the truth on the slides.

I believe we are all born with all spiritual wisdom, knowledge, and truth, and that our sojourn here is to unveil those truths and celebrate both the process and the unveiling.

Faith is the shield that prevents barnacles from adhering to my soul, but where and how do I find the evidence that creates faith?

Your Thoughts:

#23 Mom and Kings

I couldn't believe it. We were in a hotel room somewhere in Europe; it may have been Holland. Mom and I were playing double solitaire. The game requires that you shuffle the cards and deal the whole deck between two people; while doing that, you randomly turn four cards face up on the table. The intent is to get rid of all the cards in your hand by building on the turned-up cards in the middle or by playing on your opponent's turned-up card. You do not want to have Kings in your hand; they are the hardest cards to get rid of.

Mother dealt. I don't know how many cards she dealt before she turned one up, but the first one she turned up to go in the middle of the table was a King. We both cheered; that was one less king in our hands to worry about. She dealt some more and turned up the second card to go in the middle. It was a king! "Wow! Oh, my Gosh."

That was rare and really good. We spent some time enjoying the moment, then she continued to deal; she turned up the third card, and it was a king! No way! Yes, way. Were the cards marked? No. Did she peek? No? "How did you do that?" We laughed and giggled and talked about the chances of that happening. She dealt some more and turned up the fourth card, and it too was a king! What are the chances? I honestly don't know the statistical possibilities, but there it was, all four kings sitting in the middle of the table. I was in awe. That was my relationship with my mother; she was an incredibly beautiful, intelligent, strong-willed, powerful, independent, remarkable woman, and I was in awe.

Our family loved duckpin bowling. The balls are small; you hold them in the palm of your hand; they have no holes, and they weigh only 2-3 pounds. You get to throw three balls each turn instead of just two, and if a woman has an average of 110, she is considered a great duckpin bowler. Mother's average was 107. She was left-handed and had a natural hook; it was beautiful to watch.

When we went to Germany, there were no duckpin alleys; mother loved to bowl, so she decided to try out for the ten-pin bowling league though she had never stepped foot in a ten-pin alley in her life. She told them she had never bowled ten pins; they showed her how to find a ball to fit her hand; she traveled up and down the whole, long bowling alley to find what she thought might work. She bowled 211 in her very first game; they called her a liar to her face.

Mom traveled all over Europe on a special Kaiserslautern team; she never spent a dime of the family's money buying bowling balls of her own; she used alley balls wherever she went, and she maintained an average of 223.

She was opinionated, drank too much sometimes, smoked too much often; she had a great sense of humor and a hearty laugh. Her personal ethics were daunting. She was a sincere and ardent follower of her Christian faith, and she was, indeed, a "good and faithful servant." She was caring, not nurturing; she was generous, not frivolous; she was outgoing, not open. She and Dad, quietly, did a lot of wonderful work in the community. They were both well-respected in many ways. As with all of us, there was the good, the bad, the ugly, and the beautiful.

She was a life master in the Bridge World, and she partnered with some of the most famous and respected Bridge players in the world at that time. She was a staunch Democrat and a proud delegate to Jimmy Carter's convention.

I admired her; I envied her; I imitated her. I fell short of what I thought I should be and what I desperately wanted to be—just like her, but I didn't have the looks; I didn't have the intelligence; I didn't have the strength. What I didn't know; what took me a lifetime to discover was, we were alike in one very unexpected way; she was vulnerable.

#24 Finding Evidence

Faith is trust without evidence in the physical world. There are as many pathways to faith as there are people. I found four steps that work for me: (1) choosing to seek; (2) having an open mind; (3) finding the best "microscope" for me to examine spiritual slides; (4) embracing the proof I find.

Evidence is found when seeking, whether the seeking is conscious or not. I believe that we are all programmed to seek so that all of us will one day reveal to ourselves the truth of who we are. In the spiritual world, seeing proof starts with looking.

The second step to finding evidence, which leads to peace and joy and love, is having an open mind to the possibilities. An open mind does not negate the need for objectivity; an open mind merely means that all options are on the table when it comes to developing theories about the causes of events and insights we experience.

Trust is the foundation of faith that creates the ability to experience the evidence. I have heard some say that faith is belief without evidence. It is based on a biblical verse in the King James Bible, Hebrews 11: 1 *Now faith is the substance of things hoped for, the evidence of things not seen.* [5] However, belief does not guarantee trust.

Belief and trust without evidence can be an unfortunate choice at times; they can halt or postpone a person's search for proof. The most important thing to realize here is that, just because something cannot be seen, does not mean it does not exist or that we cannot access it.

Just as we use the microscope to see the evidence of entities our normal vision cannot see, creating knowledge of things formerly "unseen," we need to use a spiritual microscope to find the evidence of the spiritual things our normal vision cannot see.

I believe everyone is born with a spiritual microscope; we merely need to choose to use it. It is the same microscope we use to experience beauty. Beauty is not experienced by the senses; beauty is experienced by the spirit. Two people can look at the same sunset; one can experience beauty; the other may see only through their physical eyes and miss the experience of beauty.

I think part of the problem some have in finding evidence of spiritual truths lies in the apparent struggle to recognize the evidence when it appears. Evidence can be elusive if we are looking in the wrong places or for the wrong kinds of evidence, and so people sometimes assume that the evidence is not there. However, the evidence is there, and we will find it if we seek it, and hopefully, we will embrace it.

Imagine a person from a very remote region of the world who has never seen light produced by electricity, and I take this person to a home at night and tell him that if he were to flick this little piece of plastic sticking on the wall, the whole room would light up as brightly as if the sun were shining through every window. He looks carefully, skeptically, and thoughtfully at this little piece of plastic on the wall. How could that little piece of plastic light up the whole room? Then, he makes an important decision.

The person can choose to call me crazy and walk away, or he can choose to trust me, challenge me, or even try to prove me wrong and flick that switch. He then sees the evidence of the *unseen force* that lies within the walls of the room. Once he "sees the light," literally and figuratively, the gateway to faith in electricity has been unlocked.

I can choose to flick the switch and see the light, or I can choose to walk away from the opportunity to discover the evidence. I can choose to use my spiritual microscope to experience the beauty of the sunset, or I can walk away from the opportunity to experience the evidence I seek.

I now see so much more in John Keats's final sentence, *Ode on a Grecian Urn*. So, so much more. "Beauty is truth, truth beauty, that is all ye know on earth, and all ye need to know."[5]

#25 New York: Unfurled Joy

I was thirteen. I don't remember what ship we took, but I do remember coming into New York harbor. It seemed like thousands of people were there on the dock; maybe there were looking, waving, grinning, crying as they found their loved ones. I watched; I searched the crowd hoping to see someone I knew.

Mom and Dad had made it clear there would be no one to meet us; they all lived too far away; I kept peering into the crowd anyway. Nobody. I started to leave the deck, and Mom said, "Jeanne, look, look over there by the big, red sign. Do you see them?" There was Pam and Uncle Paul, and Aunt Evelyn, and . . . I waved, I grinned, I cried.

Joy looks funny sometimes.

#26 Increasing Faith

In seeking faith and wanting more of it, I realized faith cannot be measured in quality or size. Either I have faith, or I do not; either it is without the possibility of doubt, or it is not. I believe that is what Jesus meant when he said that the measure of faith need not be larger than that of a mustard seed—one of the smallest seeds on earth, and when you have it, not even a mountain is too big to move.

However, faith can be measured in its scope, in its expanse. After flicking the switch and seeing the light, the person who had never seen the power of electricity before may now embrace the evidence that electricity exists and have faith that electricity is a powerful unseen force in the wall, but he does not yet have faith that this unseen power exists anywhere else.

Now I take him to an automobile, and I tell him that the same power can move this huge piece of heavy metal. He cannot accept that, but he chooses to turn the key, and the car starts, and he finds that the car can be moved. He now has broadened his scope of faith. Then I take him to an airport, and to Brussels to see the Atomium, and . . .

Faith is like water pouring from an outside spigot; the water does not change in its composition or its quality. The quality of water coming out of the spigot does not change, but the puddle beneath the spigot will continue to grow as long as the water continues to flow.

Faith can grow in scope, it can expand its parameters, and once that begins, faith tends to grow exponentially. Soon it becomes evident that there may be no limit to this unseen power in our lives.

I now seek pieces of plastic to flick that sit on the invisible walls of the spiritual realm.

Your Thoughts:

#27 He Broke It

He broke the kitchen table with his fist; he would rather have hit Dad. Uncle Paul was a mild-mannered man, most of the time.

"There will be no more God damn arguing at this God damn kitchen table while we eat!" Plates flew, drinks spilled, chairs scrambled backward, and the table cracked; not another word was spoken. That's all that was ever said; that was all that needed to be said.

Mom and Dad had sold our home when we moved to Germany; we moved in with Aunt Evelyn, Uncle Paul, and Pam when we returned. Aunt Evelyn was mom's sister.

Pam and I were like sisters. We had been living together for three months; there were seven months to go before our new home would be ready.

It was a ritual—Dad picking arguments with someone at the dinner table. That night, Bobby was the target. That night, Uncle Paul ended the ritual—at least while we lived with them.

#28 Barnacle 4: Expectations and Rose

Expectations are things we think will, or should, happen. I always expected people to be on time; Rose was always late; I was always disappointed.

The parable, **Muddy Road** (p. 38), says a lot about *expectations* as possible barnacles. In the parable, Tanzan understands the expectations of a monk to love and respect his fellow human beings. Monks are expected to help others and to demonstrate the humanity that their beliefs espouse. Rescuing the damsel in distress was certainly a reflection of that element of human kindness.

Expectations can lead to judgment, condemnation, and disappointment. Ekido judged Tanzan very harshly because of his own expectations of Tanzan. It turned out that his judgment was not only wrong, but it also consumed him throughout the day, generating animosity, fear, anger, and condemnation.

Ekido expected Tanzan to follow the rule, and his expectations lead him to condemn and chastise Tanzan, and as a result of his expectations, Ekido reflects deep disappointment in Tanzan's behavior. *Disappointment comes only from unfulfilled expectations!*

It seems Tanzan did not have any expectations of Ekido; thus, Tanzan was not consumed by any negative feelings toward Ekido, nor did he reflect disappointment with Ekido's choices.

Muddy Road constantly prods me to examine my expectations just as it does my assumptions. Are my expectations more like Tanzan's or Ekido's? Do I lack appropriate expectations of myself? Do I have expectations of others that are inappropriate? Am I expecting others to act one way, and when they do not, do I become judgmental? Am I judging the heart, mind, and soul of another based on my own expectations? Am I experiencing disappointment; if so, what are my expectations? What are the foundations for those expectations?

I came to realize that I should not be disappointed that Rose is late; my expectations were out of line; there was nothing in Rose's behavior that created the expectation of her being on time. My expectation was generic. "All people should be on time," but Rose is an individual, and I needed to adjust my expectations to meet the reality of who Rose is. Rose is just being Rose. With this change in perception, I found peace. This was an important insight that has grown far beyond Rose's behavior.

I shared with Rose that it was important to me that I be on time for events, and if she wanted to go with me, she just needed to be at my place on time. If not, I would go without her and meet her wherever we were going, and I would not feel judgment, condemnation, or disappointment toward her, nor would I feel guilt for leaving her behind. She understood.

My change in perceptions and beliefs worked; I never felt frustrated, angry, disappointed, or guilty again when it came to Rose being late. Rose has since left this temporal realm, but she taught me many important lessons before she went.

She was a wonderful friend and a great teacher of spiritual awareness in my life.

#29 I lost My Identity

I couldn't find it! Pam and I frantically walked the length of the horse trail . . . twice. Without my ID card, I couldn't get into anything on the post, not the movies, not horseback riding, not the swimming pools, nothing; it was not easy to get a new one.

Bobby, my brother, came to pick us up; he was sixteen and driving. He drove the little grey Volkswagen station wagon Dad brought back from Germany.

I said, "I lost my ID card." Bobby said, "Get in the car." He drove the car along the horse trail. Pam and I were on each side of the back seat looking out the windows. We couldn't really see anything from the car, but Bobby didn't want to walk, and Pam and I were tired, we all went along with his plan.

It got stuck; the car got stuck; the car got stuck in the sand. Pam and I got out; we pushed. We pushed from the back; we pushed from the front; we pushed from the back again, all to no avail. We were stuck in the sand on the horse trail; I still didn't have my ID, it was after 5:00; it would be getting dark in about an hour.

Bobby got another brilliant idea. His summer job was running a forklift; there was a forklift just up the hill. He went up, started the forklift, and drove it down to the car to get the car out of the sand. He got the forklift stuck in the sand.

The MPs (Military Police) happen to drive by; they didn't like what they saw. They saw someone stealing the forklift.

Bobby was in the front seat of the MP car; Pam and I were in the back. Pam and I were really scared. This was a very serious situation, but for some reason, we started giggling and couldn't stop; we just couldn't. We knew Bobby was in big trouble, and we probably were, too, but we couldn't stop laughing. The more we tried to stop; the harder we giggled.

The army is very strict; when a soldier's child gets in trouble, the soldier gets in trouble. They called Mom and Dad; mom came to pick us up. Mom took Pam and me home; the MPs took Bobby to get the car and the forklift out of the sand.

On the drive home, Pam and I were still giggling until Mom turned to me and said, "This is all your fault you know; if you hadn't lost your ID card, none of this would have happened."

Nothing seemed very funny after that.

Blame can be misguided and very hurtful sometimes.

#30 Barnacle 5: The Need for Control

The need for control is indeed a tough barnacle to release. For one thing, the feeling of being in control can create a sense (often a false sense) of security. For another, being in control can, at times, be very beneficial.

Much like my expectations and my assumptions, my choices about what I can control, and *have the right* to control, as well as my reasons for needing control, serve as potentially "sticky" elements.

The only thing in life over which I have both the absolute right and the absolute power to control is my attitude, my perceptions and beliefs, my vision of and reaction to the world. In the parable *Muddy Road*, no one had control over the fact that the road was muddy; however, each had a choice as to how to handle the situation. The young lady chose not to venture into the mud; Ekido chose to ignore her plight and ultimately became a victim of his own attitude toward her and Tanzan's actions, and Tanzan chose to help the young lady cross the road, then considered his role in her life complete, and he moved on in peace.

The parable has caused me to question the things in my own life over which I try to maintain control. Why do I feel a need to have control? What would happen if someone else were in control? Why am I trying to control others or the situation? Am I reaching beyond the areas of control over which I have the right and the authority to maintain control? What am I trying to control? What benefits are there to needing to have control? What disadvantages are there? Are my safety and security emotionally, physically, psychologically, and spiritually really at risk if I relinquish my need for control? What methods do I use to gain and keep control? *So much to ponder!*

#31 I Was Lost

The kitchen chair was on top of me, and he was screaming, "Go to your room." We had moved into our new home in June; it was July. I was thirteen. I was outside playing exploring the new territory. It was an undeveloped area in the small town of Odenton, Maryland. Only six other homes had been built when ours was completed.

There were trees to wander through, a creek to explore, paths to follow; I got lost. I wasn't scared; I found my way home. I bounded in the back door joyous over my adventure.

I was greeted with silence. Being late for dinner was an absolute "no, no."

Dad, Mom, and Bobby were sitting at the kitchen table eating dinner. No one acknowledged me. I went to the sink, washed my hands, and sat down next to him.

He never lifted his eyes. "Where were you?" the military voice growled. "I was lost."

The fist flew before I said another word. I landed in the corner; the kitchen chair hit me in the face. I was sent to my room without dinner.

Lost Again

A phobia is much like an ego; it is an experience resulting from a cause hidden in the shadows of the mind.

My hands were wrapped around the steering wheel so tight my fingernails were digging into the palms of my hands causing them to bleed. I was going 50 miles an hour in a 25-mph zone. Perspiration dripped into my eyes; my tears washed it away. I bit my lip; it swelled.

I was lost.

I refused to get my driver's license when I was sixteen. After watching the films in drivers' education class, I wasn't about to get behind the wheel of a killing machine. At least, I thought that was the reason I refused to get my license. I found out later, there was much more to that decision, something much deeper, hidden far in the recesses of my subconscious, but I didn't know that then.

My parents insisted that I get my license when I was eighteen. They weren't going to take me to work anymore. I refused to allow anyone in the car with me; I wasn't about to put anyone else in danger. Eventually, I became more comfortable, but it wasn't easy.

I had exited off the beltway around Washington, DC. I was in a residential area. I was going to visit a friend from college; we were on summer break. I lived in Maryland; she lived in Virginia. I was lost.

My reaction was extreme, way out of control; I knew that. I was watching myself from some other part of me. I couldn't stop. I was hysterical with fear.

The siren blared behind me; the lights were flashing; I pulled over.

The policeman came to the window and asked for my driver's license and registration. I couldn't stop crying. I gave him what he needed. He asked why I was so upset; I told him I was lost; I handed him the slip of paper. He looked at the address; he looked at me. He handed back my driver's license and registration and said, "Follow me, I know where this is." I did. He found a place for me to park; it was not a legitimate parking space, but it would head me in the right direction when it was time for me to go home; he wrote a note and put it on my windshield so I would not get a ticket there.

I have often thought of his kindness to me. He was indeed a lifesaver; I should not have been on the road. He made it safe for everyone. I know if he told anyone what he did, they would laugh at him and tell him he had gotten conned, but he hadn't. What he chose to do protected everyone far better than giving me a ticket would have done.

Years later, when I was about 30, I was sitting in a restaurant having steak and potatoes. That meal must have been what Mom was serving the night Dad batted me back in the corner; suddenly, I was crying as that memory surfaced in my mind. I felt like a complete idiot in the restaurant, but the freedom that came from that recollection was worth every flushed cell on my face.

I understood; I finally understood. I came to realize that, on a subconscious level, anytime I got lost, I expected a fist to come out of nowhere and bat me back in a corner. I truly believe that it was that fear that caused me to wait so long to get my driver's license, why I experienced such extreme fear when I got lost in Virginia, and why it took me so many years to get a grip on the phobia—the unreasonable fear of getting lost.

Even with all the work I had done, remnants remained, but I was fortunate to have found a piece of my past that had postponed the peace of my present, but which would no longer prohibit my experience of peace in the future.

#32 Barnacle 6: The Need to be Right

The need to be right is a powerful barnacle, too. It is a very, very heavy load! Being sincerely and deeply interested in finding the truth rather than being interested in being right gives me the freedom to soar. I do not have to defend anything; I merely need to seek. Ekido carried a very heavy load all day, while Tanzan flew above the fray.

Do I need to be right? What would happen if I were wrong? Do I enter discussions needing to prove my point, or do I enter with a sincere desire to find what another person believes and why? It is more peaceful and beneficial to travel the road of genuine curiosity. *The need to be right often destroys the desire to seek.*

#33 MYF and My Mission

I don't remember going to church when we were in Germany. I started again when we came home. Pam got me involved in the Methodist

Youth Fellowship (MYF).

We bowled, had parties, and made friends. The young married couple in charge, David and Barbara, ran *Bible* study classes; we covered the whole New Testament except for "Revelations," and I joyously "reconnected" with the spirit I met when I was four.

The Spirit now revealed itself as a Soft Voice. The Soft Voice was gentle, bright, warmly alive, unconditionally loving, joyful, and wise. It was distinctly different from my voice. It is difficult to explain; it did not really have a voice quality; it was the pulse of The Spirit of Unconditional Love—*The SOUL.*

No words are adequate to describe the joy **THE SOUL** brought with it. It was alive with loving energy. I christened the loving energy *My SOUL (My Spirit of Unconditional Love)*; I did not want to limit it to a single name like Jesus, or title, like Buddha, yet giving it a name made it more personal.

After weeks of contemplation, I announced at dinner with tremendous joy and conviction, "I have decided to become a missionary!" The military voice snorted, "You don't have the personality for it." *Sadly, I believed him.*

#34 Barnacle 7: The Ego

The ego is our attachment to our human identities. All suffering comes from the ego since it is only our egos that are capable of experiencing attachment, and as long as we are attached to our ego, our spiritual identity will have difficulty surfacing.

Ekido was attached to his identity as a monk with all of the rules that go with that role. Tanzan was not attached to a specific identity; he was free to act in a spiritual way regardless of the robes he wore, the title he held, or the expectations of others.

I once saw a picture of a man standing on the side of a street looking down at his shadow on the sidewalk. He was wearing a long coat and a fedora with the brim turned down. He had his hands in his pockets; his stance was casual and comfortable. He was merely looking at his shadow, but there was something captivating about that picture. It was as though the man were examining some part of his inner self.

After reflecting on that picture, I thought—it is his ego he is contemplating, and I realized that his ego and my ego are merely shadows. It is not an enemy, though I sometimes go through life shadow boxing with it. It is not something to fear since it is not even real. It is not something to resist, nor should I spend my time resisting it; we always energize that which we resist. I merely need to move in the right direction in life, and my ego will go away.

Imagine a light shining down on me from directly above. A shadow forms only when I move away from the light; that shadow is my ego. The farther I move away from the light, the larger the shadow grows. Then, if I choose to ignore my shadow and focus on the light instead, and move toward the light, the shadow will get smaller, and . . .

When I finally step directly into the light again, my ego will completely disappear.

#35 Watching Television

The living room in our new home was too formal for a television. The family television was in Mom and Dad's bedroom; we would all pile on the bed together to watch "Gunsmoke," "Perry Mason," and "The Untouchables."

Mom was playing Bridge; Bobby was on a date; Dad and I were

watching television on the bed; I was unaware he had had an erection until he ejaculated on my red pleated wool skirt. I didn't know what was happening or why it was happening. I had merely been watching television as I always had. He said, "Look what you did" and went to the bathroom.

Without a word, not knowing what else to do, I went to my room, changed clothes, put the sperm-stained skirt in the hall closet in the pile to go to the cleaners, and went to bed. I couldn't sleep. Later, he came into my room. He was naked; he wanted me to satisfy him with my hand; I cried; I refused; he left my room. It never happened again.

I needed *My SOUL* - the Silent Voice we all can feel when we seek comfort and truth. It is the voice of the "light"; it is the voice of unconditional love. The Voice is always kind, always patient, always understanding. *My SOUL* knew I hated Dad. *My SOUL* did not condemn me. I had lessons to learn, and those lessons would be taught, but not now; the lessons could wait, now was the time to comfort. *My SOUL* helped me sob.

#36 Beneath the Surface of the Soil

Suicide has many roots—self-loathing, doubts, fears, "I'm not okay," and hopelessness. The seeds are often planted years before they blossom into the fullness of self-destruction. The roots of suicide get entangled beneath the surface of consciousness, twisting perceptions, poisoning beliefs, choking healthy roots of self-image. The buds slowly peak through like weeds on a sidewalk. The weeds seem innocuous at first, but they can, when unattended, break the sidewalk into pieces, which they did, and they nearly put my body in the ground.

I don't ever remember liking myself when I was young; my father's treatment of me helped forge a sense of worthlessness; my vision of my mother helped forge a sense of inadequacy; my vulnerability helped forge a need for isolation, and all these feelings forged the sense that I was nothing . . . nothing but a disappointment to everyone.

These roots were firmly grounded before I met Brent. After years of silent growth beneath the surface, they broke through. I realized I was going to disappoint yet more people: Brent, his parents, my parents, everyone at the wedding, everyone I knew, everyone in the world, everyone in the universe forever and ever; suicide was the only choice that made sense.

The barnacles had won. They had pulled me to the depths of the sea; I lay on the rocky bottom, then . . . fate, God, luck, all of the above, woke me from the nightmare; the gun jammed; I realized what I had done, and knew I had been given a second chance. I would not forget it, or so I thought; I would not waste it, or so I hoped; I would not let it happen again, or so I promised myself and *My SOUL*, but roots are hard to destroy, and stronger branches can grow in time.

Brent was to be in a time that had not yet arrived; right now, at fifteen, the roots were barely nudging the soil deep beneath the surface; I could not see them. Not yet.

Your Thoughts:

#37 Principals and Principles

The trouble is, if you don't risk anything, you risk even more. —Erica Jong [6]

First Grade

I was sitting outside the principal's office crying. I had gone down the sliding board headfirst; apparently, little girls in skirts weren't supposed to do that, but it was my preference; it was more fun. *Sometimes innocence gets robbed innocently in the name of decorum.*

Eighth Grade

She eyed us intently like a hawk from her strategically located "perch" in the center of the room, high enough to track us in our teams of four in our little kitchenettes in our Home Economics class. She had a rule: You must eat whatever you fix.

Frail and shy Janet fixed the chicken salad, strong but silent Carol fixed the cupcakes, cautious Louise took care of the fruit dishes, and I fixed the biscuits.

As soon as we sat down and I saw the black chicken salad on our plates, I knew we had a problem. I raised my hand.

"I'm sorry, Ms. Rivers, but we can't eat the chicken salad."

The room got very, very quiet.

Her eyes narrowed; her brow furrowed. "Why?" she squawked.

"The chicken salad is rotten," I said matter-of-factly.

She paused, "Jeanne, you know my rule."

"Yes, but the chicken salad is rotten," I said with surprise she had not understood.

"I find it hard to believe that the school has supplied us with rotten food items."

Janet and Louise started eating the chicken salad, Carol sat quietly, watching intently.

"Please, come see for yourself, honest . . ." I said genuinely holding out my plate.

She never left her perch. "You know my rule; there are no exceptions."

I looked at it again; maybe I was wrong. Jeannette and Linda were eating it.

Then I smelled it.

"Well, I'm sorry Ms. Rivers, but I'm not going to eat it; it's rotten."

She stared at me sternly and leaned forward. I thought for a minute she was going to fly down off her perch and pluck my eyes out. We all waited breathlessly for her to take flight, but she stayed there—preparing to pounce.

"Then I will give you an F," she said with great pride that she had the final say.

The tension was as dark as the chicken salad. The game of chicken was on.

I paused; I thought about it, and then with complete acceptance of the prescribed consequence, said calmly, "Okay."

I felt relieved; it was finished. I looked down and started to eat the vegetable salad. Everyone cautiously went back to what they were doing. It was over.

Then she squawked with greater severity and volume, "I will give you two F's."

There was an audible gasp; everyone froze.

After a moment or two, I picked up the dish of chicken salad; I stood and calmly walked to the trash can and scraped all of the chicken salad into the trash.

I knew the principal was calling my mother as I sat outside his office. Not a good thing. "If you get in trouble in school, expect to get in worse trouble when you get home" was the rule in our house.

By the time Mother got to school, both Jeanette and Linda had gone home sick. Mom looked at me and asked. "What happened?" I told her. She listened. She looked at the principal and asked, "The teacher never looked at or tasted the chicken salad?"

"Not to my knowledge."

"Is it true that Janet and Louise went home sick?" He confirmed they had. She looked at me and then said to the principal, "If the teacher fails Jeanne for this incident, I will do everything it takes to make sure the teacher is fired; she should be fired anyway."

I got a D in the class. The teacher was not there the next year.

A small step for me and a giant leap for my self-respect was taken that day.

Ninth Grade

I thought it was a great idea at the time; after all, how does any new tradition get started? At Arundel Senior High School, the school we freshmen would be attending the next year, the seniors had a "Senior Day." I knew that because my brother was a senior. It was a great tradition. Every senior could wear a costume of some sort to school for the day, just for fun, and to show off the fact that they were seniors.

As freshmen, we were in the highest grade in our junior high, so several of us decided that, since we were the top dog in our school, we should have a "Freshman Day."

I had a blue jumper; I took the spaghetti fringe off a pink rug and sewed it on the front to make the jumper look like a 1920s flapper dress. I then raised the hem to just above the knee and, "Aye, therein lay the rub" (to paraphrase Shakespeare). School policy was that no skirt or dress was to be above the knee.

After Mom had seen my outfit, she said, "You're going to be sent home." I could tell she was not concerned; she was merely stating a fact. Mom was a very independent and feisty woman; she challenged many rules and injustices in her life, and she was strong enough, and always willing, to accept the consequences of her actions. She saw our idea as fun and harmless, but one which was bound to have benign, but obvious, consequences. I didn't believe her, of course; after all, it was a costume, not a dress.

I didn't get past Mrs. Mitchell's third-period math class.

I waited in the principal's office.

I had called Mom to come get me. It was Monday. She said, "You'll have to wait until I finish the laundry."

Mrs. Mitchell came by the office and offered to take me home. I changed clothes and made it back to US History class.

Independence is a wonderful thing when you are willing to accept the consequences. It can build character, courage, and confidence; little did I know how much I was going to need all three to survive the next few years of my life.

#38 Forgiveness: Part I

We are all faced with a series of great opportunities brilliantly disguised as impossible situations. —Charles R. Swindoll [7]

I Couldn't

I knew I should forgive Dad; I couldn't. I wanted to forgive myself; I couldn't. I must have done something wrong, Dad had said, "See what you did?" It took years to realize the truth.

But now I was only fifteen. I had been trying ever since that night to convince myself that I wanted to forgive Dad, but today was different. I chose honesty instead.

The truth was I resented feeling I should even expect myself to forgive him; I perceived my hate and my condemnation as justified and as a punishment for him and a triumph for me. There is a lot of power in hate and condemnation; it is addictive, all- consuming, purposeful, rewarding in its sense of superiority. Hate and condemnation give birth to an insidious, destructive sense of power.

However, what I did not yet understand is that hate and condemnation always destroy the person who harbors them, regardless of whether it ultimately hurts the person toward whom those feelings are directed.

Playing victim can prove to be a self-fulfilling role; the poisonous venom of a victim's anger becomes the truest enemy of personal peace. Certainly, people can be victimized by circumstances outside of their control in the temporal world, but staying a victim is a choice; thriving on being a victim is a tragedy.

I prayed. I prayed for Dad; I prayed for me; I prayed for guidance; I prayed for peace. I prayed to forgive. I prayed to be forgiven.

Finally, exhausted and defeated, I asked, "Is forgiveness even possible?"

There was a palpable shift in the air around me when I asked that question. My racing thoughts screeched to a halt. I felt *My SOUL* smile, and I found myself going back in time to when I was playing in the sand.

The smile gave me comfort again, and I assumed the smile meant, "Of course, it's possible to forgive"; I found out later, I was wrong. Yes, wrong.

I find it amazing how often assumptions turn out to be incorrect.

#39 Transcendentalists: The First Step

Minds are like parachutes -- they work best when open. — Thomas Dewar [8]

A Cup of Tea (Repeated)

Nan-in, a Japanese master during the Meiji era (1868-1912), received a university professor who came to inquire about Zen.

Nan-in served tea. He poured his visitor's cup full and then kept on pouring.

The professor watched the overflow until he no longer could restrain himself. "It is overfull. No more will go in!"

"Like this cup," Nan-in said, "you are full of your own opinions and speculations. How can I show you Zen unless you first empty your cup?"[2]

The longest journey begins with a single step; I took mine in American Literature class in my junior year. I didn't know that it was my first step; I just knew that the Transcendentalists took me to places I had never gone before, yet those places felt so familiar, and I wanted to continue to go back.

Emerson

1. "Of the universal mind each individual man is one more incarnation." [9]

2. "Everything the individual sees without him corresponds to his states of mind, and everything is in turn intelligible to him, as his onward thinking leads him into the truth to which that fact or series belongs." [10]

3. "Whoso would be a man, must be a nonconformist." [11]

4. "A foolish consistency is the hobgoblin of little minds . . ." [12]

5. "Nothing can bring you peace but yourself." [13]

6. "Our faith comes in moments; our vice is habitual." [14]

7. "A man is a façade of a temple wherein all wisdom and good abide." [15]

8. "... *that Unity, that Over soul, within which every man's particular being is contained and made one with all other; . . . Meantime within man is the soul of the whole; the wise science; the universal beauty, to which every part and particle is equally related; the eternal One.*" [16]

The Over-Soul, that's what Emerson called it: The Over-Soul. I knew immediately what he meant. Each time I read him, I felt like I was talking with an old friend about our favorite topic. He believed there is eternal, infinite truth to be found in all things of the material world; we merely need to look. He knew *My SOUL*.

Thoreau at Walden Pond captured my emotions, and my desire to seek outwardly and inwardly. The Transcendentalists sent me on a journey I have yet to complete, and I don't ever want to end the trip.

An open mind is a doorway to freedom.

Your Thoughts:

#40 Forgiveness: Part II

It is not the mountain we conquer but ourselves. —
Edmund Hillary [17]

I had not yet been ready for the lessons *My SOUL* wanted to teach me, but now I was willing to empty my cup without spilling my principles; to see things in the light of truth without being blinded by them; I wanted to be forgiving and forgiven; the problem was I didn't know how.

Now, it was time; the student was ready, and the teacher started speaking. *My SOUL* gave me a homework assignment. I was to study how Jesus handled forgiveness. Ah, how wise, *My SOUL* wanted me to start with what was familiar; something I could understand and trust. I went to work immediately.

The research proved startling, to say the least.

I got out my well-worn King James Version of the Bible, I sat on my bed, and I read all the incidents in which Jesus forgave. I studied them carefully. I read each one many times. I looked for patterns, insights, wisdom, and guidance.

What I came to understand was, very honestly, quite disturbing at first. The insights I gained were a contradiction to what I had always believed; they were, actually, a complete contradiction of what I thought forgiveness was. What I had thought to be the truth in the past I discovered was indeed misleading, and what I initially saw as unbelievable, turned out to be a truth. Ultimately, what I felt was joy.

The smile I had seen when I had asked, "Is forgiveness even possible?" flashed before me. I had misinterpreted that smile. The smile meant that I had precariously stepped onto the precipice of understanding but was not quite ready to peer into the beauty below. I had come to the very question that leads to truth; I just needed to be ready, ready to get beyond the traditional way of viewing forgiveness, ready to discard old assumptions, ready to step out of the box and over the edge.

I needed to look from above instead of from below, and then I would see the way to freedom from my pain.

#41 "Strange" How Things Happen Sometimes

Senior class Vice Presidents don't do much; that's what I discovered after I was elected. It felt good to be popular, but that was totally insignificant compared to the other events of 1963.

There was a popular comedian, Victor Borge, who created a comedy routine called, "Phonetic Punctuation." It was the verbalization of punctuation. He would talk and make popping sounds with his mouth where a period would go. He had a different sound for commas, question marks, exclamation points, colons, and semi-colons. It was a very funny routine.

In the first semester of my senior year, two of my classes were British Literature and Public Speaking. One assignment in British Literature was to memorize and write down a Shakespearean sonnet with proper punctuation. At the same time, in speech class, our assignment was to present an entertainment speech; I had no clue what that meant.

I was fervently marching up and down the living room floor dramatically reading out loud, sonnet XVIII, "Shall I Compare Thee to a Summer's Day?" To facilitate the memorization of the poem, I was incorporating Victor Borge's phonetic punctuation.

Mother walked in and started laughing really hard. Mom had a great laugh. She suggested I do that for my entertainment speech. The night before the speech was due, mother's idea suddenly seemed like a great one.

Ms. James, my speech teacher, loved it. She offered extra credit if I would do it for the school variety show scheduled for November 29th. I said, "Okay."

On the Friday before our show was scheduled, November 22, 1963, President Kennedy was assassinated. The shock was devastating. Time stood still. Nothing else was important. Everyone was glued to the television trying to absorb what we were seeing. Events all over the world were canceled; no one can move when they are numb. The grief was palpable everywhere.

It was not until Wednesday of the next week that the school decided our variety show would *not* be canceled. They decided the show must go on. The community supported the decision. The auditorium seated over nine hundred. It was packed. My life was changed.

I did the skit; nearly 1,000 people laughed genuinely and loudly; for five minutes they forgot their sorrow, the shock, the pain, the loss. I touched them, and they touched me. I knew from that moment on that theater was to be a major part of my life; touching people through acting became my mission.

I would be a missionary after all.

Your Thoughts:

_____

_____

_____

_____

_____

_____

_____

_____

_____

_____

_____

_____

_____

_____

_____

_____

_____

_____

_____

#42 Forgiveness: Part III

The greatest discovery of any generation is that human beings can alter their lives by altering their attitudes. — William James [19]

When the Student is Ready . . .

I was a diligent spiritual student of *My SOUL*, a willing student; I was spiritually fertile soil ready to embrace the seeds of understanding, but I could never have been prepared for the lessons *My SOUL* intended to teach me. I had studied the four Gospels of the *Bible*, reading over and over the times Jesus spoke of forgiveness. Many insights flew through my mind; the first was the most startling of all.

Insight One

Jesus never forgave! If the *Holy Bible* is an accurate accounting of events, Jesus never forgave anyone. Jesus always said, "Your sins are forgiven"; he never said, "I forgive you." The more I studied the scriptures, the more obvious it became. Jesus made a deliberate choice not to say, "I forgive you."

As I reflected on this insight, I began to wonder whether I was splitting hairs. Did it really matter how he expressed it? Was it a coincidence that his words were documented as being the same nearly every time? Was it an accident that I had come to see this fact?

I concluded I was *not* splitting hairs. I knew there had to be a purpose in the way he expressed himself. I knew I had been led to this insight, but I didn't know why.

Did the fact that Jesus never personally forgave mean that I did not have to forgive Dad? That thought excited me; it would certainly make my life a lot easier if I did not have to forgive dad, but the truth was, that idea did not ring true to me. I knew the lesson was not complete; there was more to understand. Why did Jesus never forgive?

Insight Two

The second insight came, and it seemed so obvious once I received it, that I remember being "tickled" at its simplicity. Jesus never forgave because he never condemned. Jesus never forgave because he saw nothing to forgive in anyone. The phrase, "Your sins are forgiven," was his way of saying the sins had already been forgiven, had always been forgiven, had been forgiven even before they happened, would always be forgiven because sins are never perceived by God.

Jesus did not forgive those who nailed him to the cross; he did not need to; he had not condemned them. In saying, "Father forgive them for they know not what they do," he was speaking to his fellow Jews who believed that God judged and could provide forgiveness, but I believe he knew that their God had not condemned them. Jesus had seen past the assassins' actions; he had seen past the conditions; he was aware that "they knew not what they were doing." Their fears, their anger, their actions were not the core of their problem. The core of their problem was a spiritual identity crisis, but I wondered how that insight related to my life.

Was I supposed to believe Dad did not know what he was doing? I could not accept that idea! His actions were deliberate on his part. I was a bit peeved at *My SOUL*!

Then, the Voice of *My SOUL* said the following, "For they know not what they do" really means, "For they know not who they are." That hit me like a brick. *For they know not who they are.* That's a huge difference. His assassins were spiritually ignorant, spiritually unaware of their true identity. They had forgotten who they really were; had they remembered their true identity, a child of God, unconditionally loving wisdom, they would not have done what they did.

Ah! so, did that mean Dad had forgotten who he was, forgotten his spiritual identity, forgotten that he was a child of unconditional love? Now, that struck a chord of truth, and I could forgive someone for forgetting who they really are; I realized I, too, had forgotten who I was.

Insight Three

The third insight was both frightening and exciting. It was frightening because it contradicted everything I had ever thought about forgiveness; it meant I had to view forgiveness from a completely different perspective. The insight seemed bizarre, yet uplifting; *My SOUL* said, "Forgiving is not something you can do."

I heard that statement, and questions flooded my mind. Forgiving is not something I can do? But isn't that what Christianity is all about—forgiveness? Isn't that what most religions are about? How can it be something we cannot do when that is the primary thing we are supposed to do?

"Forgiveness is not a verb; it is a noun. Forgiveness is a result. Forgiveness is not something you can do; forgiveness is the result of what you stop doing," the voice delivered that powerful fact swathed in a warm, genuine smile. "When you stop condemning, forgiveness happens." *My SOUL* paused for a long time; it knew I needed time to reflect.

Then the voice continued. "The need to forgive is conceived in the womb of condemnation. Condemnation is something that has to come first in order for there to be a need to forgive."

I immediately wrote that down, and I said it over and over. "Forgiveness is a noun; it is a result. Forgiveness is not something I can do; forgiveness is the result of what I stop doing; when I stop condemning, forgiveness happens. The need to forgive comes from a perceived injustice. Condemnation is what I have done first in order for there to be a need for me to forgive."

It was true; I was condemning my father for his actions. The message was that I must first stop condemning, and then forgiveness would happen. It became obvious to me that it is impossible to forgive that which I am still condemning.

It is possible to pardon, which is to relinquish punishment or consequences while still condemning, but it is impossible to forgive while continuing to condemn.

I was trying to forgive Dad and forgive myself when what I needed to do was the opposite. I needed to relinquish condemnation, then forgiveness would happen. I had kept trying and trying and trying to forgive Dad and me, but I found forgiveness elusive. Now, I knew why.

Insight Four

When I love unconditionally, forgiveness is never necessary. That was lesson number four. In the world of unconditional love, there is no need for forgiveness because there are no perceived injustices; there is nothing to condemn; thus, there is nothing to forgive.

So, if I did not condemn my father, I would experience forgiveness of him.

But . . . how do I relinquish condemnation of things that I know are wrong?

Your Thoughts:

#43 Where Was Mom?

Your pain is the breaking of the shell that encloses your understanding. —Kahlil Gibran [20]

Dad had been in World War II. On the day he returned home from war, Dad beat Bobby, who was only three, for having an accident in his pants.

I was four when Dad went to Korea for a year, but what I remember most is what happened just before he left. They didn't know I was standing in the kitchen doorway; I was not very imposing at four. "You didn't have to hit me," Mom said.

I was sixteen when I learned about their "agreement": Never contradict each other's discipline in front of the children. Mom kept her word, but I knew she was busy doing what she could to protect us without undermining Dad's authority.

She often defended him to me in a feeble attempt to smooth things over. "After all, he did quit smoking." "He thought you were being a smart-aleck when you said you were lost." "He just didn't want you going off to the jungle to be a missionary." I understood; it didn't work.

Mom had her own war raging; my problems were mere skirmishes; I knew that.

#44 Good or Bad?

Who Knows What is Good or What is Bad? —A Taoist Parable

. . . an old Chinese farmer lost his best stallion one day and his neighbor came around to express his regrets, but the farmer just said, "Who knows what is good and what is bad."

The next day the stallion returned bringing with him 3 mares. The neighbor rushed back to celebrate with the farmer, but the old farmer simply said, "Who knows what is good and what is bad."

The following day, the farmer's son fell from one of the wild mares while trying to break her in, and he broke his arm and injured his leg. The neighbor came by to check on the son and give his condolences, but the old farmer just said, "Who knows what is good or what is bad."

The next day the army came to the farm to conscript the farmer's son for the war but found him invalid and left him with his father.

The neighbor thought to himself, "Who knows what is good and what is bad." [21]

Only the end can reveal the meaning of an event. I genuinely believe we all have a happy ending, and so every event is moving us closer to our final victory.

#45 Cheaper by the Dozen

After performing in the Variety show, I tried out for the Senior Class play, "Cheaper by the Dozen." Ms. James was directing. I did not get cast.

I went home, told Mom, and cried. She said, "You don't have to be in the play to be a part of it. Why don't you see how you can help; maybe you could help paint the set, or work on costumes. There's a lot to putting on a play."

I went to every rehearsal. I helped with the set and the props. I filled in for people who missed rehearsal. Diane Chamberlin had been cast in the lead; she got sick a lot. I filled in for her so much, I practically knew her whole part.

Two weeks before opening, Diane announced she could not do the show. Ms. James was going to cancel the show. The cast asked her to put me in; she did.

Mom said we could have the cast party at our house. Ms. James came. I told her I knew I didn't do as well as Diane would have done, but I did my best, and I enjoyed doing it. She said, "You did far better than Diane could ever have done." Wow!

I wanted to major in theater; my parents said no. I had to listen; I didn't have the money to pay for college myself. I didn't like their decision, and I resented it. I had been bitten by the theater bug, and the fever never died.

Theater was going to be in my life; it just was not going to be my major. I majored in Psychology, minored in English, and had a wonderful life teaching for more than thirty years, and I still found many ways to make theater a consistent and vital part of my life, even today.

"There is nothing either good or bad, but thinking makes it so." [22]

Shakespeare was so wise.

#46 Forgiveness: Part IV

Say not, "I have found the truth," but rather, I have found a truth." Say not, "I have found the path of the soul." Say rather, "I have met the soul walking upon my path. —
Kahlil Gibran [23]

A Vital Conversation

My SOUL asked me: "Does something which does not harm you require forgiveness?"

Me: "No." I knew where *My SOUL* was heading, so I said, "But my father's actions have harmed me."

My SOUL reminded me gently, "Remember who you really are."

What follows is my best recollection of the lessons I derived from the whole conversation I had with *My SOUL* that day.

Lesson one: The real "me" is pure spirit, the spirit of unconditional love.

Lesson two: My spirit, everyone's spirit, is invulnerable.

Lesson three: Everything that happens in the earth realm can be used to bring enlightenment - awareness of my true identity—and the peace and joy that accompany that awareness.

Lesson four: If something works for my good, then it is not harmful.

Lesson five: All things work together for my spiritual well-being when I choose to discover, savor, and digest the nugget of unconditional love that is securely nestled in the nucleus of every event in my life.

I contemplated the lessons long and hard. I wanted so much to understand them and to apply them in my life. I went over them and paraphrased them and examined them from every angle my young, inexperienced mind could find.

I came to understand that if I look at every event in my life through the prism of unconditional love, then I will see everything as either a way to live unconditional love or as a pathway to finding unconditional love; every event becomes good no matter how bad it may look through my physical eyes, my mind's eye, or my heart's eyes. If I live in the spirit of unconditional love, I will see only the positive in each event in my life.

If I, or Dad, or anyone else, commits a "sin"—we have merely missed the mark of unconditional love. We miss the mark when we lose sight of who we are. I had come to understand that a moment of confusion needs compassion, not hate. If I, or Dad, or anyone else, misses the mark, it is because we are coming from fear, and that very moment needs love, not anger. When we miss the mark, we have forgotten who we really are, and that very moment in our lives is worthy of understanding, not retaliation.

I chose to see things differently. I chose to see the actions of my father as wrong in this realm, but to see him as a child of God in need of love. I chose to no longer condemn him, just his behaviors. I chose to see my father as a Buddha in my life, there to teach me about unconditional love. To teach me that it is easy to love that which is lovable, but when we come to love that which *seems* unlovable, we have reached Nirvana. I began to see that dad was teaching me about unconditional love not by what it is but by when it is needed most.

I had come to realize that I energize that which I resist, so it is best not to resist that which is not of love for I will energize it. It is best to resist feeding my own fears or the fears of others, for I will energize them. I had come to understand that the only antidote to that which is not love is love.

I had come to understand that if I reflect love in the face of fear I will see the truth in that reflection, and I will remember who I really am once again. I wanted to always remember: "All things work for my spiritual well-being when I choose to discover, savor, and digest the nugget of unconditional love that is securely nestled in the nucleus of every event in my life."

The messages seemed so over-whelming then, but in the ever-fluid spheres of time, I found tranquility in their clarity, joy in their freedom, and peace in their wisdom.

I felt tremendous relief for the first time since that night of watching television. I was proud of myself. I believed I had taken a giant leap in my spiritual life.

My SOUL hugged me gently and smiled, and chose to keep from me, for the time being, that what I envisioned to be such a huge leap was barely beyond a crawl, and that even at that, I was crawling at an angle, which would miss the mark if I kept that path.

I had yet to learn that "relief" is an infinite number of beliefs away from peace.

Your Thoughts:

#47 Michael and the Letter

It was eleven o'clock on a Tuesday morning in the summer between my freshman and sophomore years at college. I was lining up typing paper and carbon paper in the typewriter; the floor fan was blowing and creating major problems; the temperature was in the high eighties; I was working in a virtual hotbox on the Ft. Meade, Maryland Army post. I didn't look up when Michael came in; I was too focused.

I typed the paperwork for the reserve troops who came in for two-week summer training; the officers in charge would come and go out of the isolated building all day. They all kept an eye on me since I worked there alone; I felt very safe.

His shadow loomed over my desk; the shade felt good; then his well-sculpted, smooth hand reached down, held the paper in place, and I scrolled; he was a Godsend.

I looked up and fell in love with his smile. He came back later and brought me some lunch; that was our first meal of many that summer. We went for a lot of walks in the evenings; he knew his constellations well; Orion was his favorite; I knew them very little; I made Orion my favorite. He taught me a lot. We laughed a lot. He held me a lot.

He knew how to handle me; I wasn't easy. I wanted someone strong, and yet I wanted my independence. I didn't know enough about my own sexuality, so I thought I wanted a man; Michael was all man.

I never met his folks; they lived in Texas. We spoke of engagement before he left, but we never did anything formal.

He wasn't suited for Viet Nam, but neither were a lot of the young men who went. He was a physics major, tall, dark, and handsome except for the dark brown wart on the tip of his nose. He was happy, lanky, and not very coordinated.

It was seven o'clock the night before his unit shipped out. I was not supposed to; no one was allowed to, but I did it anyway. I went to his barracks.

I had to do it; I had to give Michael my gold cross. He was Catholic, my cross didn't have the crucifix, but I had to give it to him anyway. I knew the guard on duty, and I talked him into finding Michael; he did.

I gave Michael my cross and said, "Bring this back to me." We kissed; I said good-bye.

He wrote as often as he could. He found ways to keep the letters light; he laughed at himself; he was the only officer in the vehicle when he fell off the back of the truck; they never let him forget it. He was well-liked and respected.

I was home from college recuperating from mononucleosis when I had the dream.

It was a vivid dream, in color. I dreamed one of my letters to Michael came back with "Receiver Deceased" stamped in red ink, in a circle, on the envelope. I had never seen or heard of that; I thought it was my fever.

I went back to school; the letter was on my desk. I didn't cry; it didn't seem real.

Two years later, on a Friday night, I saw Orion and sobbed for three days.

> *God, grant me the serenity to accept the things I cannot change, the courage to change the things I can, and the wisdom to know the difference.* —Serenity Prayer

#48 Self-Awareness

If we try and fail, we have temporary disappointment.
If we don't try, we have permanent regret. —Bern
Williams[24]

The trend of my benign independence continued in college. I didn't join a sorority; I was not in their league; it was not my style.

Greek week bothered me. It wasn't "fair" (so I thought) that during Greek Week, only fraternities and sororities could participate in the Greek Week variety show. (Now that I reflect on it, my thinking was flawed.)

I marched into the organizing committee's office, pled my case, and, for the first time, they opened the variety show to any group that wanted to participate.

Ten of us became the "Simpson Hall Singers"; we all lived in the dormitory of that name at Frostburg State College (now, the University of Frostburg). We sang, "I Believe" and "Cockeyed Optimist." I directed; we took third place, made school history, and got a plaque on the wall in the Simpson Hall lobby. I wonder if it is still there.

I have since lost my attachment to a need for fairness, not my appreciation of fairness, but my need for fairness; that is part of my movement from crawling to standing on my feet, but that evolution would not develop for several years to come.

College was hard; my grades showed it.

It was a Thursday night, my junior year. I called home and announced that I was quitting. Mom was very wise; she did not resist; she merely asked me to think about it over the weekend; if I felt the same way on

Monday, she and Dad would come to get me.

I assumed I would be packing over the weekend.

Friday morning, I rushed down the steps of the home where I was staying; several of us were now living in town. I was out of breath when I answered the phone. The voice on the other end asked, "Is Jeanne there?" I asked, "Which one?" My roommate's name was Jeanie. The voice was familiar, but I wasn't expecting the Dean of the college to be calling me, so I didn't recognize her.

Dean Manicure was a no-nonsense dean with a good heart. She said she had been meaning to call me to let me know how much she enjoyed the Simpson Hall Singers. She also remembered that I had won first prize in the college variety show with my Victor Borge routine. She mentioned how much she enjoyed the concerts that *Collegium Musicum* put on each year; she knew I was a member of that elite choral group.

I told her how nice it was of her to call; it meant a lot. She asked how I was doing. I told her the truth; she paused and said, "Oh, Jeanne, I really hope you don't quit."

She told me the school needed me, that I was an inspiration, that I broke barriers, changed traditions, and made a positive impact; she loved my independent spirit and thought my influence was very important. Dean Manicure had done her homework well—factually, and psychologically.

Monday, I called Mom and told her I had decided to stick it out. Years later I put two and two together. Mom must have called the Dean; it was just too much of a coincidence. Mom never told me that she called the Dean, but she often did things very unobtrusively, with no fanfare, no cry for attention, no need for accolades—just quiet, powerful, important, life-changing actions.

A stumble may prevent a fall. —English Proverb

Your Thoughts:

#49 The Incident

*Of the good in you I can speak, but not of the evil. For
what is evil but good tortured by its own hunger and thirst?*
—Kahlil Gibran [25]

I had gone to Texas with Pam. She was meeting her fiancé who was stationed there. It was late at night; I decided to give them some time alone. I went to the motel swimming pool. I was raped by a man I didn't know; I was still a virgin at nineteen.

I didn't report the rape. I was from out of town; we were in a cheap motel; girls were not believed then; I concluded nothing would come of reporting it.

I became pregnant. Abortions were not legal except for fringe circumstances; mine was one of them. The process was a trying one. I was in college; it was miles away from the military hospital I was entitled to use. I took the train; it took hours. I took public transportation; it took patience; I called my brother; it took courage.

The process required me to pass the exams of two psychiatrists to qualify. The abortion required induced labor and delivery. The first time it was scheduled, I arrived only to discover that it was too soon; I had to be further along. I had to go back to school and wait some more. By the time the procedure was performed, I was three and a half months pregnant.

I killed a child; there's no way around that. I begged the doctor to tell me if it was a boy or a girl; he refused. I'm glad; he spared me the burdened of thousands of images of the *might-have-been*s, but the sorrow lingers.

Another tragic awareness came to me as a result of this event, and it shook me to my soul. I came to realize I had it in me to kill someone; I could have killed him. I would never have believed I was capable of such a thing. It was something I needed to learn about myself so I could heal that possibility.

#50 The Lock

Fear is the little darkroom where negatives are developed.
—Michael Pritchard [26]

I had arrived home from Texas. It was my first night home alone. It was time to go to bed. I went to the front door to lock it.

I reached out for the bolt; I came to a dead stop just before my hand touched it. A crossroads; a fork; a decision. I paused. I had never locked my door before; there had never been a reason to.

I clenched my jaw. "No! No! No! I will not become a victim a second time." I had been his victim once, but I didn't have to remain one. He controlled my body for a time, but he would not control another moment of my life."

I had a choice; go through life with fear or go through life with love. I didn't lock the door; I slept through the night for the first time since the rape.

The secret of life isn't what happens to you, but what you do with what happens to you.

#51 The Ouija Board

Vision is the art of seeing the invisible. —Unknown

It was in her dorm room. Jeanie Crawford, my roommate, and I had gone to visit Nancy. It was near the end of our junior year. Nancy had an Ouija Board; it was new to most of us. I was watching from the top bunk, enjoying the proceedings, convinced it was rigged.

It came to my turn. I had no idea what to ask, so I asked the first thing that popped into my head, "Will I be back next year?" I figured that question would be an easy "Yes" and my turn would be done.

It said, "No."

I laughed. I had gotten through the worst of times; I was determined to graduate now; I was sure my "partner" on the Ouija Board was playing games. I went along. I said, "It must not know who's asking. Let me ask again." "Will I, Jeanne Sanner, be back to Frostburg State College, in the fall of 1967?"

"No."

"Okay, okay." I looked at Nancy who had her hand on the Ouija Board with me. "Okay Nancy, I'll play along." She said, "I'm not doing it. I'm not moving it, honest!"

"Okay, Ouija, then why will I not be coming back to Frostburg in the fall?" "Baby."

Well, everyone cracked up at once. They all knew I was one of the few virgins left on campus. I knew, then, without a doubt, Nancy was playing around.

"Okay, okay—I'll bite—who's the father? "Don't know," said the Ouija

"Oh, come on Nancy, at least give me a hint. Do I know him already? Will I meet him this semester? Is he good-looking? Is he a good lover? Do you know him?"

She said, "Honestly, I would never have come up with any of this!"

"Okay. I'll try one more time, and that's it for me. So, Ouija, you don't know who the father is? I thought you knew everything! Why don't you know who the father is?"

"Rape."

I went to Texas with Pam that summer and sat by the pool.

Your Thoughts:

#52 Forgiveness: Part V

It is only through the womb of truth that forgiveness can be born. —Jeanne Sanner

Sanity versus Insanity

Forgiveness lives just beyond unconditional love. Some might say that it is insane to choose to forgive, to relinquish condemnation, but if we start seeing things differently, we will see unloving behaviors as cries for our help, that plead for compassion, and love, rather than seeing something worthy of our anger or fear or retaliation.

When we respond to an attack with compassion and love, we find peace and joy. That may seem impossible, but if I just remember to empty my cup of fear and to know without doubt, (faith) that it is indeed possible to see the world without condemnation, I will find the truth, the way, and a life of joy. It became important to me to place a permanent wedge beneath the door to unconditional love so I can walk through into its peace at any time I choose.

The Amish

On October 2, 2006, an armed gunman entered an Amish school, killed five young girls, and then killed himself. What the Amish did next is a marvelous example of how it is possible to see the world without condemnation.

1. They chose to comfort not only one another but also the wife and children of the man who had been responsible for such loss.

2. Though they could not understand the events in this man's life that led him to such a horrendous action, what they believed is that the killer had not come to know God's love, or he would

not have been able to do what he did. In other words, he did not know who he truly was.

3. The Amish offered compassion to the wife and children of the killer; they invited the killer's family to the funerals of the girls and attended the funeral of the murderer.

4. Some of them knew the man who had done this, and they said that they were sad that they had not been able to help the killer find the peace and comfort of a loving relationship with God.

5. Their perceptions, their beliefs were: "We think it's all in God's hand . . . If you have Jesus in your heart and he has forgiven you . . . [how] can you not forgive other people?" (ABC News, October 3, 2006).

In their sorrow, they found comfort in their souls; in their confusion, they found peace in their faith; in a world filled with rage and retaliation, they found compassion in their hearts, and the whole nation—no, the whole world was moved.

Finding unconditional love a little "peace" at a time is an evolutionary process in which my ego diminishes, and *My SOUL* becomes more visible. *My SOUL* does not become stronger as my ego diminishes; it becomes more evident. Just as at night, the light of the sun is not visible, its power, its brilliance is not diminished - *My SOUL*, our souls, are not diminished when we walk in shadow; their light does not dim.

Our souls are pure; they have always been pure, and they will always stay pure; they have merely been obscured in the midnight of our fears. The true nature of *My SOUL* becomes more visible as I step back into the dawn of my awakening.

#53 Summer Stock and Taking Stock

A brook would lose its song if God removed the rocks. —
Barbara Johnson [27]

There were no auditions. The director just handed me the script for *Stop the World I Want to Get Off* and said, "You're Evie." It was the summer of 1968. I had finished my course work but had to do my student teaching in the fall. I always worked during the summers while going to college, but my folks agreed that I could be in the summer stock program instead; I was thrilled.

I started to devour the script I knew nothing about. I couldn't believe it; Evie was a key character. I kept reading; I stopped in my tracks. I ran into Anya, parenthetically it said, ("Evie"); I read further, Ilse, ("Evie"), Ginny, ("Evie"). Did that mean . . .?

Each of the four parts had a different accent; Evie - British; Anya - Russian; Ilse - German; Ginny - Brooklyn, NY. Fortunately, accents came easily to me.

Summer stock was hectic, tiring, exhilarating, never-ending, intensified learning. We did five shows concurrently. Besides being the lead in "Stop the World . . .," I was in the chorus of "Carnival," worked on make-up for the children's show, "Flibbertigibbet," costumes for the comedy, "Sunday in New York", and was Assistant Director for the drama, "Look Back in Anger." I worked on the sets and built two steps from scratch that actually held people as they danced on them!

I hated letting people down; it happened. I wasn't up to the task in the role of Evie. The primary roadblock came early in rehearsals. The director wanted "Littlechap," the male lead, to lay on top of me to symbolize the affair he was having with Anya. The rape was still too raw.

I asked for the blocking to be changed, but it couldn't be. I went inward. The director understood, but that didn't help. I couldn't relax; I couldn't break free; I couldn't bring the character to life the way I wanted and the way I knew the director wanted.

We had performed the show twice; I got a lot of compliments, but I knew that I wasn't doing what I could. I wanted to break free of the chains that were binding me. I wanted to rebel against my fears.

My Comforter, *My SOUL*, came to visit. In our heart-to-heart chat, *My SOUL* reminded me why I had wanted to get into theater in the first place. It wasn't about me at all; it was about touching people. I needed to forget about my fears, my needs; myself; I needed to let the love of people and the love of theater be my guide. I needed to go toward love, not resist my fear; resistance energizes that which we resist. Choose to go toward, not away. I needed to risk—totally risk—and trust that I would not be alone.

I found a safe and solitary place to rehearse and fought for a breakthrough. I belted my songs and focused on the characters.

The next performance night came quickly. I did it; I risked; I trusted. I forgot about me. I lived "Evie" to the fullest; I connected with "Littlechap" like never before; I projected my songs like never before; I owned the stage like never before, and I loved it. My ego was lost in the souls of "Evie" and "Anya" and "Ilse" and "Ginny."

We had barely finished our curtain calls when the director was standing beside me. "What happened to you?"

"Good or bad?" I asked. He couldn't contain his grin, "Incredible; absolutely incredible." I said, "Thank you," and left it at that.

I kept my Comforter close and my ego at bay for the rest of the summer. It was an incredible graduation ceremony for the college education of *My SOUL*.

#54 Guilt: Part I–Thanksgiving Dinner

Student teaching went well in the fall of '68. I graduated in January of '69, married Brent in July; left Brent in November; moved in with Ann, the sister of my brother's best friend, and Ann's roommate, Donna. My emotions were raw, but I was relieved. I had yet to grasp that there are millions of miles between relief and peace.

I didn't expect it. I went to my parents' house for Thanksgiving. I walked in; Brent was sitting in the living room. He was alone for the holiday; Mom felt sorry for him. I was blindsided. It was too soon. I was still battling my own guilt and trying to heal my own wounds. I needed their understanding and their support. I felt betrayed. Brent's feelings were more important to them than mine. I had expected my parents to be more sensitive to my needs, more loyal, more respectful.

Expectations can ruin the taste of turkey. Guilt can ruin the taste of life.

Tenacity

My feelings of guilt were the result of my inability to relinquish condemnation of myself for my culpability in creating what I perceived to be negative consequences for Brent and everyone else and for my homosexual inclinations.

Guilt is one of the most tenacious barnacles alive. It devours peace and joy; it sucks the love out and replaces it with fear and remorse. It weakens me; I sink; it thrives.

There must be a way to release guilt's attachment.

#55 Instruments of Navigation

Sailors have many wonderful instruments to help them navigate the seas. They have a sextant to determine locations, a compass to indicate directions, maps to plan their course, charts to guide their decisions, and shipmates to share the journey.

I needed instruments, too. I needed honesty with myself as my sextant to discover my location in the sea of life. I needed wisdom to give me direction. I needed principles to plan my course, I needed trust in *My SOUL* to be my North Star in guiding my decisions, and I needed companions to share my journey.

I started my new voyage completely <u>unprepared</u>.

#56 Barnacle 8: Assumptions

I was on my own, sort of; a person is never alone when she lives with two other women. Diane was a physical education teacher; Ann taught History. I got a teaching position at Northwestern High School teaching senior English.

I was consciously wrestling with my sexuality; leaving Brent because of my physical attraction to a woman forced the issue. I didn't know Donna or Ann before moving in, but when they asked questions, I threw caution to the wind and chose to share the truth, the whole truth. They seemed to understand; at least, they were accepting and were without judgment. That was a tremendous relief since I didn't understand myself yet, nor was I accepting of myself. Their attitudes were therapeutic.

I couldn't be sure; I didn't know much about being a homosexual. I hadn't even ever been aware of meeting one. I did assume Donna might be a lesbian; she seemed "butch." That was the extent of my "understanding." Nothing was ever said to me about them. I sensed no sexual attraction between the two of them; I assumed Ann was straight.

I was lying in bed. Donna was out, and Ann came into my room. She did not turn on the light. She asked me if I was awake, and when I turned to answer, she lay on top of me and kissed me. I pulled away and told her to get off me. She did. "I thought you wanted it," she said. She left the room; nothing more was said or done.

Why did she think I wanted it? Did she expect me to welcome that? I had no attraction to her. I had not indicated that I was interested, at least not to my knowledge.

What signals was I sending? How many other people were receiving these signals? I was confused, so I had an affair. Unfortunately, he was a married man.

I met him at The Baltimore Comic Opera. We were in "Little Mary Sunshine." He was a gentle soul, small in stature with a big heart. I didn't know he was married; he never wore a ring. After he had fallen in love with me, and I had fallen in like with him; he told me the truth.

I was devastated, not because he wasn't available, but because I had participated in something I didn't agree with. I told Frank we had to tell his wife. We did. It was one of the hardest things I've ever done. I never saw him again. Years later, he went to my parents' home in search of me; they gave me the message; by then, I knew who I was; I didn't call him back.

Frank was the first, but not the last. There was "Judd" in the production of "Oklahoma." There was the traffic cop who asked me out instead of giving me a ticket. There was David, who was the friend of a friend, then there was . . . never mind, it doesn't matter. The trysts didn't change my sexual orientation; I couldn't morph my way into something I am not no matter how many men I went to bed with.

The frivolous relationships ended, but the guilt did not.

My Mirror

The world constantly provides me with situations from which I can learn valuable spiritual lessons; the key is to recognize those situations as opportunities instead of seeing them as obstacles to my intentions.

When Jesus said to the prostitute, "Go and sin no more," he was saying, "Go and remember who you are; you are the invulnerable, holy child of the Most High."

My SOUL is the mirror that shows me who I truly am
when I remember to look at my reflection.

Your Thoughts:

#57 " . . . and the ankle bone's connected to the . . ."

The Drama teacher decided she would not direct the senior class musical production. The senior class musical was a long-standing tradition at Northwestern High. When she made her decision, it was too late to order the materials for the traditional shows: *South Pacific*; *Carnival*, *King and I*; *Oklahoma*.

The students were angry and disappointed; they came to me. I asked them what they thought they could do; they said, "We'll write our own musical."

The principal said, "No." He did not want to take the chance that the show would be a flop and that it would be worse for the students than having nothing. After a little persuasion, the principal said, "Yes," but for only one weekend instead of the traditional two week-end fare.

They were at my bachelor's apartment every spare minute we had. One loved writing while lying, fully clothed, in the bathtub; one picked the only closet I had; another was in what was called a kitchen; the rest of us were all over the living room.

We had to pick music that was over fifty years old to avoid royalties; they called their show, "Those Were the Days." They wrote a delightful musical about the 1920s.

We picked the songs and got the music to the band/orchestra teacher so they would have time to prepare.

Finally, opening night arrived, and it was a whopping success! By popular demand, we got a second weekend of performances. Mom and

Dad came; they loved it.

Two other people whom I did not know came; Tim and Mary Jones; they loved it. They needed someone to direct a play for a charity they were supporting; they asked me; I accepted. I chose Lillian Hellman's *Autumn Garden*.

I wrote a promo for the County Newspaper; the editor called to ask who wrote the promo; I told him; he asked me to lunch; he offered to pay me to write a weekly theater column for the County newspaper; I did, "Back Stage with Jeanne Sanner." I got $5.00 per article.

The column led me to a Community Theater group, the Aldephians, located in Adelphi, Maryland. I directed "The Fantasticks" for them, which led to Goddard Space Station's MAD (Music and Drama) group, which led to Darla, which led to the lead in "Once Upon a Mattress," which led to the lead in "My Fair Lady," which led to . . . and the knee bone's connected to . . . *My SOUL*.

"All the world's a stage, and all the men and women merely players . . ." [28] The theatre is one of my favorite places to be. I have learned so much about life there, physically, emotionally, psychologically, and spiritually.

#58 Guilt: Part II–Pretend with Me

As the curtain opens, the set is revealed. The stage is stark. The audience sees a tiny kitchen in a basement apartment. There are no windows; the lighting is dim; there is a small table with only one lamp that creates shadows on the faded, peeling wallpaper.

A 1950s phone leaves little room for the beer bottle by the lamp. There is a card table for a kitchen table with empty whiskey bottles, drained glasses, dirty dishes, food scraps, and crumpled napkins. There is one empty chair, a distraught, haggard woman is slumped in a stupor in the other. A beat-up refrigerator seems to thrust itself into the room to escape the smell of the greasy countertop. A broken wooden door hangs on one hinge just below the chipped porcelain sink; two crusted pots cling to the sticky stove and an oval, worn-out rug attempts to create some warmth but fails. (A bit dramatic, huh?)

Though this set is solid and three-dimensional, it is not real. It is an illusion. The door stage-right does not really lead to the hallway outside the apartment; it leads to the wing of the stage. The phone does not really ring; a technician creates the sound. The light switch does not really turn on the lights; a technician does that, too. The refrigerator does not really keep the food cold, and the stove does not really create heat.

But the actors go through weeks of rehearsal pretending the set is real; they answer the phone; they flick the light switch; they turn the knobs on the stove. It becomes their world; they adjust; they react; they live and even "die" in this mirage of crime and punishment.

The lights on stage slowly, inconspicuously grow a little brighter. A gruff, angry man enters stage right. He starts a violent confrontation with the woman in the chair. His intensity is palpable, and the woman's submission is heart-breaking. He kills her.

An FBI agent tracks him down and kills him. The last scene is in the mortuary. The audience knows the murderer is lying in the casket. No one else is in the room. The curtain comes down. There is a dramatic pause; then the audience jets from their seats, applauds loudly, and shouts "Bravo!"

Behind the curtain, the killer climbs out of his casket and gets in line with the other actors for a curtain call. They take their bows; the audience goes home; the actors stay a few minutes to have their pictures taken, and then the battered wife, the murderer, and the FBI agent all go out to dinner and celebrate their performances.

There is no guilt, for no one is really hurt. They have a wonderful evening together with no thought of the anger and hate their characters felt towards each other just hours before. Their lives go on in peace and harmony until the curtain goes up the next night, when our antagonist will confront again and kill again and die again.

Healthy actors know how to keep their true identities separate from their illusory selves, but sometimes actors get so involved with their character, they start taking on the traits and characteristics and perceptions and beliefs of that character, and they lose a part of themselves. If they are continually "typecast," they can lose a lot of their own identity, not only for the public but for themselves as well. They can become as depressed as the characters they play, or as much of a victim as the ones they portray, or as much of a hero who saves the day—and that situation is where and when the trouble begins.

In this physical, temporal realm, I am the total accumulation of my perceptions and my beliefs; it is those perceptions, thoughts, and beliefs that create my emotions and my actions. When I am my spiritual Self, my perceptions are without threat, they are without condemnation; my faith is without doubt; my emotions are without fear, and my acts of kindness are without boundary.

However, as I get more and more involved with the "character" I have chosen to play in this drama called life, I introduce more and more attack thoughts, fears, and actions that are contrary to the spiritual Self I really am. I move out of the spiritual spotlight that shines directly overhead and into the shadows the spotlight creates as I move away from its glow.

Metaphysically, Shakespeare's metaphor of the world being a stage works well in describing where I am, how I got my identity, and why I have trouble separating myself from the world so that I can be in it but not of it.

My ego's identity can get lost in the drama of earthly life. Spiritual unveiling is about reconnecting with my true Self and then staying true to that Self while continuing to live in this world.

The theater serves as the foundation for my ultimate understanding of what is meant when people say this world is an illusion. Everything that can change is part of the illusion; only that which is timeless is real: spirit, unconditional love, wisdom, peace, joy, and freedom.

My Play; My Option

My SOUL was providing the laboratory for me to explore, experiment, and come to understand that I can choose to accept a different role, one which more accurately reflects who I truly am, one that is without guilt, and one that would change my whole concept of reality.

But my conscious awareness of that concept would not surface until years later.

#59 Ralph

We met in "Oklahoma" in Maryland. Ralph played "Will Parker." I was the musical director and orchestra conductor. My dad had been a professional musician and bandleader; he taught me a lot about conducting, but experience taught me more.

I had been in choruses since junior high; I was in a chorus in college; I had directed the Simpson Hall Singers in the Greek Week variety show; I had never conducted an orchestra, but that job came with the territory when I agreed to be musical director for Mary Jones's production of "Oklahoma" at the Goddard Space Center.

Ralph never knew whether he would be scampering two steps a second or casually strolling through his solo, "Kansas City." Sometimes after the chorus was finished with their portion of the song, I would stop conducting; the orchestra members patiently reminded me that they still had music to play after the chorus stopped singing; we laughed a lot; I learned a lot; the show was a rousing success.

Two men came up to me after one performance and said, "We thought it was just a stunt to have a woman conductor, but you are the real thing!" That was a baffling statement to me; I never thought twice about the fact that I was a woman; what did that have to do with anything?

I will never understand pre-judgment.

Ralph is gay; he was struggling, too. He couldn't reconcile his sexual predisposition with his religious beliefs. He was fighting it; a gallant fight it was, too, for a while. We became very close; we moved in together. He was the best male lover I ever had. Eventually, we both faced the truth. It wouldn't work. It wasn't supposed to. I moved out; he finally pursued his passions. I was not ready yet; defining ourselves isn't always easy. Ralph and I are still very close.

#60 Relationships

Life is all about relationships, relationships with others and ourselves, physically, emotionally, psychologically, and spiritually, and our relationships with the world and God. Some relationships are more difficult to reconcile than others, like the relationship between war and unconditional love. Viet Nam is still a haunting specter.

However, spiritual truths have a way of reconciling the irreconcilable, providing peace in the midst of war, preserving joy in the midst of sorrow, and making the meek much stronger than the mighty. The spiritual world is upside down, or is it really right side up?

If I reverse the order of priorities in Maslow's pyramid of Hierarchy of Needs, I will see the spiritual world's hierarchy. I will see the pyramid Jesus and Gandhi and Buddha and other spiritual teachers built; their hierarchy reverses what is perceived to be real; physical needs are last and least, instead of first and foremost.

If I combine my awareness of the fact that I live in many different worlds concurrently with my awareness that the physical world is like a stage and that, after the curtain comes down, we will all be united, sitting at the same table, sharing laughter and love, then I can move beyond my dad's abuse. I can move beyond the rape. I can move beyond Michael's death. I can move beyond the horrors of war. I can move beyond judgment and condemnation. I can move beyond guilt, and I can find that idyllic peace that "passeth" all understanding; the kind of peace that reaches far beyond my comprehension, far beyond Maslow's pyramid and into the sacred chambers of the pyramids built by the spiritual masters of the world.

Spiritual truths are pathways to peace.

If only I could traverse them when I need to the most.

#61 The Visitors

Two men knocked on the door of my classroom; I went out into the hall; they flashed their Federal IDs. They asked about Brent. I said only wonderful things. Brent was applying for a position that required a government background check; two divorces raised a red flag. I made sure they understood; Brent was one of the most outstanding men I had ever met. They left; I was glad I did something positive for him; he deserved it.

I felt more than relief . . . I felt at peace.

An act of kindness helped loosen the clutching barnacle of guilt over Brent, but there was so much more I needed to learn before I could ever experience the absolute freedom that we are.

#62 All Things Work Together

The student knew better; his parents didn't and neither did the principal. I was called into the principal's office to discuss the student's final grade; he had failed senior English; he couldn't graduate. The principal asked me to review the situation. I did so gladly. I got my grade book, pointed out all the assignments the student had failed to do, and though he was a bright student, there was no choice but to fail him; he had not met even the minimum standards.

The principal asked me to change the grade. I refused. The parents had power; the principal changed the grade; I resigned. I was out of work again.

The student heard that I resigned; he found me; he apologized for his parents; he knew he had failed. He showed more integrity than his parents and the principal.

I said something to him I had remembered from Methodist Youth Fellowship, *Holy Bible* (Romans 8: 28), "All things work together for the good."

Little did I know then where my new path would take me and how true that statement was going to be for me.

Your Thoughts:

#63 A New Life

The next fall, I got a job teaching English and Psychology at a different school. I was in my late twenties, living completely on my own, and choosing to work diligently on healing emotionally by doing what I loved. Professionally, I loved teaching; for fun, I loved community theatre, and for my true Self, doing what I loved most deeply - seeking spiritual wisdom and truth through extensive reading and contemplation - broadening my spiritual temple to include the wisdom of all the major religions of the world.

Since high school, I continued to pursue spiritual wisdom from every corner of the world. I loved, and still love, experiencing the *Autobiography of a Yogi*, the *Bhagavad-Gita*, the *Upanishads*, *The Holy Bible, Tao Te Ching*, and *The Prophet*. I became enthralled with studying Islam, Judaism, Buddhism, Taoism, and more.

Siddhartha Gautama of the Sakyas, Carl Jung, Edgar Cayce, Ken Keyes, Ralph Waldo Emerson, Henry David Thoreau, and many other extraordinary poets and authors came alive in ways I had not experienced. It was intense and life-changing.

I was advancing slowly, but I was traveling along the road to well-being. I was exploring my inner world with the joy of an astronaut exploring new worlds in space.

I was living in a high rise perched snuggly atop a hill on the fifteenth floor with a beautiful vista overlooking a small town below, surrounded by woods with a lively stream: Private Hill Apartments - paradise.

One enticing summer night, I went out on the balcony to soak in the view. I had been reading *The Prophet*. I was content; the lights in the homes below were twinkling like the glistening stars above, and the warm, comforting night air was gently stirring.

There was peace in the evening breeze, and love. As I looked down over the little cluster of houses, I was overcome with a desire, an intense, powerful longing, an aching to just reach down and touch every single person in every single home and assure them all that they are loved with a love greater than they probably had ever known. But as much as I longed to do that, I knew I couldn't.

It was a desire Jesus would have had were he standing here. Strangely, as I thought about what he might see and feel, I became acutely aware of his pain, his greatest pain. I stood there stunned to suddenly realize that the greatest pain in Jesus' life was not what he had suffered on the cross. His greatest pain was, instead, the pain of knowing that, in his limited time on earth, he would not be able to reach down, or out, or into every person's heart with the love He and God felt for them. He ached with an ache beyond human experience.

I began to feel that pain, that agony, that desperate sense of despair. How great His pain must have been if someone like I, who cannot love as He loved (and loves yet today), could feel this tremendous heartache. I began to cry for Him and for His pain. I knew what He had really wanted, and I knew He knew that He could not have it. I wept; no, I sobbed alone on the balcony.

When I finally achieved some semblance of self-control, I decided to go back inside. I was empty and sad; I didn't know how to comfort the one who always comforted me, though I knew His days of sorrow had ended. I came in, turned around, closed the door to the balcony, and turned back to enter my living room.

I took only five or six steps when I looked up and stopped. I stared; I blinked. I found myself gazing at a brilliant, warm, beautiful, golden light, glowing in the corner of the room directly across from where I was standing. I had no fear; in fact, I was drawn toward it naturally, instinctively, and the light grew rapidly in size and in strength blanketing the room as I approached.

Then we merged, and I found myself engulfed in the most magnificent, powerful, unconditional love that I had ever known. I was overwhelmed; all I could do was fall to my knees and cry, but this time I cried with joy; I was sobbing again, but free from pain and sorrow. I was filled only with light and love. I felt the glow pull me in and cradle me in its bosom; I *felt* a gentle voice comforting me, and I knew, I *knew* that I was loved unconditionally, completely, totally, eternally, and infinitely. The physical world disappeared; there was only God holding me in His arms.

When I finally emerged into conscious awareness of the physical world again, drained and yet invigorated, I knew two things without doubt:

We cannot abide for long the full power of God's love in these fragile vessels. It is more than one's body can bear; it is greater than one's mind can fathom; it is deeper than one's heart can feel; it is the expansive essence of THE SOUL. I also knew that love far greater than ourselves is always there to cradle us and give us peace.

This was, and has remained, the most sacred moment in my life.

#64 Disappointment

The next four years went by quickly, as they always do when we are busy. I found myself acting, directing, and conducting orchestras in Washington, DC, Baltimore, and Virginia; teaching, working during the summers, and constantly reading spiritual materials of all kinds.

It was in the spiritual arena that I felt defeated.

Disappointment comes only from unfulfilled expectations; I had expectations of myself that were unfulfilled and have remained, in some respects, unfulfilled yet today.

I did not share my experience with the light with anyone for years; it was too sacred; it was too moving; it was too personal. Ultimately, I shared it with Ralph; I knew he would believe me; he would honor the moment; he would understand my disappointment.

I had expected a much greater change in me after that experience. I expected to be wiser, kinder, more loving, more at peace, and more everything spiritual. How could I go through that and not be completely changed? Why would I be granted such an experience unless I was to do more with it? I had been moved beyond words; I knew how much I was loved, yet I went about my daily life with very little change in my activities, my relationships, or my spiritual exploration. I wanted, with everything I did in life, to reflect what I had come to know; instead, I stayed very much the same. I wanted desperately to change, to be different, to be better.

Ralph was no help; he loved me just as I was.

If only I could do the same.

#65 Knock and It Shall Be Opened unto You

The knock on my classroom door startled everyone. All my students froze and watched carefully to see what I would do. I had a reputation; everyone on campus knew I did not like interruptions of any kind—from the intercom, the door, or even fire drills.

I quietly, firmly, calmly walked to the door and opened it; there stood Laura.

She could not spit her words out fast enough, "I know you hate interruptions, and I am really sorry, but I need to get this paperwork in right now. I was wondering if I could be your assistant for third period? I need you to sign here, if that would be okay?"

Shock! Laura had been a student in my previous semester's Psychology class for seniors. She was an "A" student. I thought she hated me. It was rare for me to have cause to think any student hated me, but I had called on her randomly once; she scowled and snapped an answer so abruptly that I never imposed on her again without due cause.

Too stunned to think; I signed the paper; she reported the next day.

Third period was a sign-language class (Signed English); I had designed it over the summer. During the first semester of the year, I went through all the appropriate channels and got the course approved as an elective for second-semester senior-class students. It had never been taught in our school system before; to my knowledge it had never been offered in our state.

There really wasn't much for a student assistant to do in a sign-language class. There were no simple quizzes to help grade, or papers to file, no items to organize, no photocopying to do, but she needed to have the slot filled. There was no grade involved with being a student assistant, so it all seemed strange; what do I do with her? So there we were, both a little uncomfortable.

I think it was about the third time she came to class that she stood at the door, before the bell rang, while the students were coming in and said to me in a very serious tone, shaking her head in total frustration, yet total innocence, "My mother and my grandmother need a divorce!" I still laugh out loud when I think of that moment. I didn't know her story yet, so I'm not sure why, but that statement struck me as one of the funniest things I had ever heard. My laughter instantly tore down all my barriers and assuaged all my concerns about how well we were going to work together for the semester; I loved her humor.

In time, I learned Laura's story. She was an illegitimate child who had never known her father but was never really drawn to finding out anything about him. Laura was loved unconditionally by everyone in her family, and her uncle served as a wonderful male role model for her; in fact, he was the coach of the community, summer, girls' softball team Laura was on.

Despite the unconditional love of her family, Laura had defenses; she was a very attractive girl but a little over-weight and had experienced the typical and cruel behavior of young people. Despite her size, she was an outstanding athlete as a softball catcher, and she coached a young girls' basketball team. She won athlete of the year, but boys are not usually attracted to athletic girls in high school. I was glad I was there for her so she could open up to someone.

Laura was a wonderfully caring and giving person when she felt safe. I remember she would leave class early and go to the cafeteria for me. Faculty had only 25 minutes for lunch and by the time we got to the cafeteria and to the faculty lounge, there was barely time to eat. She would bring her lunch and mine to the classroom, and we would sit and chat and have a leisurely lunch instead of a hectic one. That was a great gift.

About half-way through the semester, Laura asked me, since I was not currently involved in a show, what was I doing after school—besides grading English and Psychology papers. I shared with her that I was taking a Bible study class.

That's when I learned that Laura had not really been raised "in a church" or any particular religious philosophy. She had gone with a friend now and then to a Methodist church and had decided to be baptized after being persuaded by her friend that it would be important, but her greatest source of information about religion, at least Christianity, was from the musical *Jesus Christ Superstar.* She knew the words to every song and was passionate about the story.

I decided to ask Laura if she would like to go to that class I was taking; she said yes. We met for dinner at the Ranch House with plans to go to the class. Other than with Ralph, I rarely shared in any detail all of the spiritual explorations I was doing in my life; most everyone I knew was entrenched in their Christian beliefs, so talking about Nirvana or Krishna did not seem to fit in very often, but I found myself sharing these things for the first time with someone who was interested in hearing about my discoveries.

Having to articulate spiritual concepts is a challenge; I welcomed it; I learned from it; I grew from it, and so did Laura. I was not trying to influence Laura, nor was she at all moved by my discoveries—Laura was (and still is) very much of the physical world; I was of the spiritual, but she was an excellent listener, and the conversation provided delight for me and insights for her; I love win-win situations. We did not make it to the Bible class that night; we had our own spiritual discussion over a great steak dinner, and it was wonderful for both of us.

After that, we would periodically get together for dinner, and she would sometimes come over to my apartment where I would share different books from the, now large, library I had developed. She found a few books of interest to her, but not a lot. I admired and respected her independent thinking.

Prom Night

Prom night was around the corner and Laura did not have a date. I called a former student of mine; he graduated from Potomac three years earlier. I often kept in touch with my former students, and Michael was one of my favorites; in fact, we are still close friends today; we talk several times a week and get together when we can, and he was a huge help in editing my first book. I asked him if he would escort Laura to the prom and go with Ralph and me; Ralph often filled in for me on just such occasions. Michael accepted, Laura was thrilled, and a grand time was had by all.

Graduation

It was time for me to say good-bye to all my seniors. I loved teaching, and the key reason was that I loved my students. They kept me young, though I wasn't that old; they kept me on my toes, though I was pretty limber; they kept me laughing, and I did the same for them. There is no profession like teaching.

Laura graduated in June 1978, and the summer break began.

The Knock

The knock on my apartment door startled me; I wasn't expecting anyone. I said, "Come on in." (I still was not locking my door.) I looked up, and there was Laura. Shock!

"Hi!" I said somewhat startled. "Is everything okay?"

"Yes, I was in the neighborhood and thought I would stop in; I hope you don't mind."

"No—it's perfect timing; I have nothing planned for once."

I tried to hide my discomfort, and I had hoped that I was successful.

Love Was in the Air

For the past ten years, there had been no time in my life for any romantic or physical relationships. I was not drawn to anyone and had no time to think about it. I did not need it, but mostly I was still uncomfortable with my sexual orientation.

I was teaching; I loved it. I was living alone; I embraced it. I was active in theater; I thrived on it. I was continuing my spiritual journey; I was ensconced in it. I had experienced "The Embrace"; I was grateful beyond words for it. I was in a carefully designed protective bubble of platonic love with the world.

I doubted I would ever get involved with anyone again; my sexual orientation seemed in conflict with the Christian core of my now eclectic belief system. The scope of my faith had not grown large enough to encompass my true nature. *My SOUL* had never condemned me, but there was still the guilt, always the guilt. How many ways can I be a victim of my own guilt?

There had been times when I sensed Laura was flirting with me, but I suppressed the truth of that, and I suppressed my very strong attraction to her, to her mind, to her soul, to her body.

I had maintained my adult responsibility and distance in the relationship; after all, she was a student, and I was in a position of authority, not to mention that she was eighteen and I was thirty-two—how silly is that! How crazy is that? Had I not learned?

Could I not find someone my own age? The questions. The guilt. Always the guilt.

I had hoped that she would never discover my attraction for her; she had graduated; she was gone—or so I thought.

There she stood at the door, blue eyes sparkling, smile glistening - radiant - in all her glory to me.

I invited her in, tried to be casual, tried to be calm; we were sitting on the couch, I turned to say something to her, but she held my face in her hands and gave me the most powerful kiss I have ever experienced in my life.

She maintained her advances; I resisted.

She leaned in; I gave in. She moved in.

Forty-four years later, we are still together and still in love.

Your Thoughts:

#66 Guilt: Part III–Ralph

Ralph moved that year. He called and said we should come, too.

In September of 1979, I quit teaching; Laura quit college; we followed the setting sun across the country to Seal Beach, California, and moved in with Ralph.

The freedom to love Laura without restraint was breathtaking; the guilt was overwhelming. Laura is an only child raised by her grandmother and mother. She was the apple of their eye, their joy, their purpose; I took her away to California. Laura felt it, too; we repressed the guilt; it would, with great force, surface later, but for now, there was this irrepressible bond and desire to be free to live our lives; California seemed to welcome us, so we began a new adventure and a new life together.

Living by the ocean was wonderful; the weather was perfect. There was a feel of freedom in the air, but there was also the practicality of finding jobs and getting settled into a new lifestyle; my savings were not going to last long; that was certain.

Laura had not liked school in Maryland, mainly because she was not yet sure of what she wanted to pursue, so she went to work at McDonald's and as a maid in a local beachside hotel. After investigating the public-school systems, I realized there were more hoops to jump through than I was willing to do, so I got into sales. It seemed life was falling into place, but . . .

Not All Was Smooth Sailing

It was less than a year before it happened. I didn't know why; I didn't know how. Where did it come from? Why had I not seen it coming? Why had I not felt it coming?

It was this incident that led me—no, drove me—no, forced me to look into the mirror of my little "s" self, the ego. I knew I needed to reflect on who I was and how I had gotten there.

Ralph came through the door a bit disheveled and disturbed; quite unusual.

"What happened?" I asked with my normal alarm and concern.

After Ralph explained that he had fallen off his bike and hit his head, my fear for his safety started insisting that he go to the emergency room right away. He resisted.

My ego determined that I knew better and that he could have a concussion. He resisted. My beliefs that concussions are serious and need to be tended to, surfaced to push him a little harder to get him to go. He resisted.

My expectations were that he would listen to me. He resisted.

I assumed when I picked up the car keys, he would follow me out the door and let me take him to the ER. He did not move.

I knew I was right; why couldn't—why wouldn't he see that? He did not move. My ego insisted on taking control, I simply told him he was going to the ER.

He suddenly yelled loudly. "**S**top it!" I had never heard him yell; I had never seen him so angry; I had never been frightened around him before.

I went to my room and looked into the mirror of my psyche and became horrified by what I saw. I glimpsed an unforgettable image; I was "covered in barnacles." Fears, beliefs, assumptions, expectations, the need to control, the need to be right, my ego, and my guilt—they were peppering my "self" like ugly pimples oozing their poison into my life.

How did this happen? How could I fix it?

It was a long and winding road that had led me there, and it would take another long and winding road to lead me out.

Laura and I found a place of our own on Ocean Avenue and 13th street.

It was then I realized that Ralph was not the only victim of my fears and my guilt.

#67 Guilt: Part IV–Laura

A different kind of fear and a different kind of guilt arose in me. I was raised in an abusive environment, and I started to see those patterns developing in me. Out of the bowels of Dachau and Paris, a deep-seated fear of abandonment rumbled and began to spew out onto the surface of my subconscious. Fear of losing my relationship with Laura arose from the ashes of a burning desire to protect what we had; a fear that she, too, might abandon me, became a dominant part of my perceptions of my world.

I became controlling; fighting to ensure safety. I had not yet come to know that only freedom can give birth to safety. Safety suckles only on the breast of unconditional love. I did not like my anger. The fear grew, so the ego grew, so expectations, assumptions, beliefs, rules, and boundaries grew, and so the guilt grew, and so the fear grew more, and the ego grew more, and the expectations, assumptions, beliefs, rules, and boundaries grew more, and so the guilt grew even more, and this is the house that fear built on sacred ground, having pulled my house of love asunder.

Though Laura seemed immune, I knew she could not understand why I had become the way I was now. At this point, neither could I. What had happened to all of my spiritual studies and awareness? What had happened to the safety I felt in the arms of *the soul*? Where did the fear come from? How could I replace it with the love I knew I still was—somewhere deep inside.

Laura was raised in an environment of unconditional love. She never knew anything violent; her family never raised their voices; never cursed at each other; never attacked each other physically, emotionally, or psychologically, never pounded on tables, or punished with a strop. She did not have times in which her father (whom she never knew) chased her down the street with a knife as when my father chased my brother down the street with a knife, or my Uncle Leo brought a gun to the Christmas Eve family gathering. I had tapes—horrible tapes from my childhood that needed to be erased, and I didn't know how.

I was never physically abusive with Laura, but my fits of anger, though always directed at myself or a situation, not her, still had to be difficult to contend with on some level. After any incident of displaying raw fear, I would feel guilty; Laura didn't deserve to be around that level of anger, self-hatred, lashing out, and acting out. How could I harness all the fear in me and all the guilt? Guilt for being born, guilt for being less than I should be, guilt for being in a relationship I constantly questioned spiritually, yet, a relationship of love so deep and so real, a love I had never known before Laura, a love I could never let go of.

I thought of getting counseling, but I had been there with Brent before I left him. I wanted to work on my relationship with Laura another way. I knew I had to change my whole circuitry, and Laura would have to be a vital part of that change if it were to be a permanent part of my life, so I ask her to help me, and she did.

Whenever I acted in a way I did not like, I would stop myself. I had asked Laura not to stop me; I needed to recognize things for myself. Then, I would walk around a chair, or leave the room and return, and start the conversation over again, determined to re-program my behavior patterns. Laura was always patient; she was always aware that I was doing the best I could; she never criticized; more importantly, she never took on the victim role! Those tapes were persistent, and my changes came slowly. I cannot count the number of "do-overs." I often wondered why Laura stayed, but she loved me unconditionally, and I was blessed by that.

We have often said she was in my life to teach me how to love myself, and I was in her life to teach her how to love her fellow man. Though Laura was raised with unconditional love in her home, the world had not proven to be as kind. Laura always was bigger than her peers; she was heavier, and she was teased because of it, so she created a wall, a very thick wall, a very tall wall, an extraordinarily strong wall. It was the wall I saw when I had called on her in class; it was a wall I respected. It was a wall she invited me to climb over; I did, and we are both blessed by that.

Your Thoughts:

#68 The Strangest Arrangement

It was, and still is, the strangest rental situation I have ever experienced. There was an apartment building near the beach in which there was a really small, one-bedroom apartment that got "passed down" from one person to another with just one instruction: Send a check for $250.00 to this person (a woman's name was provided), at this address once a month; when you move, give the next person the key and the same instructions.

We did just that. We never met the landowner; we never signed a rental agreement; we never put the apartment in our name; we never paid the utilities since no bills ever came to the apartment. We mailed a check and moved in. The place was filthy, the plumbing leaked, the carpets were grimy, the walls needed painting, there were no drapes on the windows, and the light fixtures were broken.

Laura and I treated the apartment as if we owned it. We found bright, happy wallpaper for the kitchenette, bought drapes, cleaned and cleaned and cleaned some more, painted the walls a nice soft green, and got the plumbing fixed. Finally, it was not only livable; it was cozy.

We had lived there just six months when it happened. It was between 11:00 and 11:30 pm; we were watching the nightly news. The noise was coming from outside our apartment, and it sounded like someone was fooling with the meter reader for the electricity.

I opened the front door, looked down the walkway, and there he stood, wobbling a bit, in the dark, staring at the meter. I said, "Excuse me, can I help you?" He stumbled toward me, and I could smell the liquor several feet away.

"Yeah, you can move!"

"Excuse me?" I said confused, frightened and rebellious.

"I said, you can move. I am about to inherit this property from my mother; she can no longer manage the property, and we don't allow pets, so you and your dog can move out." He said all of that with a glee I certainly did not understand.

"Would you like to come in and explain?"

"No, you heard me."

I said, "But you don't even know us; why not give us a chance here?"

"You have a dog. They ruin property; they carry fleas; they pee on rugs."

I tried one more ploy. "Please come in and see this apartment. We have worked our fingers to the bone to make this place nice; it was a disaster before we moved in; if we were the type to let a dog make a mess in the house, we certainly would not have invested our time and money in cleaning the apartment up, and we have sent the rent every month."

"Oh, I know what you have done to the place; I have been watching you for months."

Then I got mad! He knew all that we had done with our own money and time, yet he was just going to throw us out. It was his right, but it wasn't right.

I said as politely as I could muster, "Could we please make an appointment to talk about this before you make your final decision?"

He agreed. He came by the next day; he was sober, apologetic, appreciative of how well we had taken care of the apartment and said we could stay, but that we could not have any additional pets, and if this pet were to die, we could not bring in any more.

It wasn't long before Kahlil (named for Kahlil Gibran), our much-beloved sheltie, became paralyzed in her back hips, and we had to say good-bye. She was twelve; I do not suspect foul play; hip problems are normal for that breed; it was just her time to go.

Laura said she wanted a cat; we weren't supposed to, but we went looking, and that's the day we found Mira (short for Miracle). She was anything but a cat, she was a 35-pound sheltie- German Shepherd mix, she had the same tri-color markings as Kahlil, and she was the only one not barking in the pound as the rain came down; I still remember the pathetic expression on her face—a face no one could have said "No" to.

We notified our landlord, gave him a 30-day notice, and moved. The move changed our lives in ways we never could have imagined.

It is rather ironic that Mira turned out to be the impetus for a string of events that led to the greatest miracle of our lives, but I am getting ahead of myself.

#69 Jingle Delight

We loved the new apartment complex. There were only thirty-three apartments; the pool was in the middle of the rectangular design. We moved to a one-bedroom on the second floor, but we kept our eye on the two-bedroom, two-story condos that were a part of the complex hoping one would become available.

Mira was a welcomed member of our family and soon became part of the apartment complex family, and then we took in another member. One of our neighbors had cats, they had kittens, we fell in love with the little one; it was near Christmas time, and so we adopted *Jingle*. I was not a cat person, or so I thought; however, we soon found out that Laura is allergic to cats, but it was too late—Laura and I had already gotten attached. Jingle was a short-haired cat, and if Laura didn't put Jingle near her face or rubbed her eyes after petting her, everything was fine. I kept the house clean and kept windows open as often as possible.

Christmas was always a fun time in the complex; everyone celebrated Christmas whether they were Christian or not—we got into the decorating mode, and it always looked like a little Disneyland by the end of the Thanksgiving weekend.

Life was good. We managed to push aside doubts about the spiritual validity of our love, or at least we had pushed them down deeply enough they didn't slip into our conscious minds. We had a dog, Mira; we had a cat, Jingle; we made lots of friends; we lived a normal life. I made strides in minimizing the impact of my tapes. Laura finished her RN degree, passed her exams, and had a full-time nursing job—an important dream fulfilled. I was a successful sales manager for a long-distance phone company.

One of the friends we made, Lynn, was involved with a local community theater; she told me about auditions coming up for *To Gillian on Her 37th Birthday*. I auditioned, got a role, and found an actor's family at Westminster Community Theatre. Soon I was directing *The Mousetrap* for the group and loving it.

A condo opened; Laura and I moved to the other side of the swimming pool; our attached garage opened out to the parking lot; everyone came through our home on their way to or from work—Angie, the complex manager, who became a wonderful friend, jokingly said we should charge a nickel to everyone who came through—we loved the energy; we loved our life. All was well . . . for the moment.

#70 Guilt: Part V–Darla

Darla never spoke to me again; my guilt was unbearable. No matter how many spiritual lessons I learned, life just kept on giving me more.

We had many friends come to visit us in California. Darla, Dave, and their son were some of them.

I was still in Maryland when I met her; I had not yet met Ralph or Laura. It had been nearly a year since I had done any acting or directing. Tim and Mary from the theater troupe, *The Adelphians,* asked me to audition with them for Goddard Space Center's upcoming production of the musical comedy *Once Upon a Mattress*. I did. Darla was the director. That was the first time we met.

Darla was one of the most unique individuals I had ever met. She was a petite four-foot-eleven powerhouse! She had naturally curly, wild, and wiry brown hair; she would shave her legs dry; she was highly intelligent and determined to have her own way.

My audition went badly; other than the senior class play, it was the first time I had auditioned; all other roles had been handed to me, but Darla saw something in me she wanted for the role of *Winnifred*, the lead. She told me to meet with Gil, who played the piano, and go over the songs. I did; it didn't help; my old insecurities had returned full bore; I went home defeated and embarrassed.

I was standing on the balcony feeling sorry for myself, when *My SOUL* "tapped me on the shoulder."

"It is not about you, Jeanne; it is about the audience." There it was again; life is not about me—it is about extending to others the love that I am.

I ran out of the apartment and headed straight to the stream; a place of solitude; a place to belt out a song without reservation; a place to be free. It worked. I blew everyone away (including myself) when I auditioned one more time and got the role.

Our Friendship

Our love of theater was our common bond; Darla was, and is, one of the most important individuals in my life. We were both strong, though she was stronger; we were both direct, though she was blunter; we were both talented, though she had more experience; we were both courageous, though we were bold about different things; we both had a good sense of humor, and we both had different points of view on quite a few aspects of life, but one thing was sure, we were friends for life, or so I thought.

The Fantasticks

It was 3:30 in the morning when we finished. Darla kept saying, "I can't believe we're doing this. I can't believe we did this!" But I knew I had no choice, and there was no one else I would have called at 10:00 pm on a Thursday night to help me do it.

Success breeds success. A small, local dinner theatre invited me to direct *The Fantasticks*. It was Thursday night; the show was opening Friday. I had hired someone to do the lighting design; I hated it. I decided to change it. I had never designed lighting, but there I was on stage saying to Darla who was on a ladder, "Change the middle Fresnel's gel to blue; widen the range; increase the intensity to level three; I want the angle of the number six Fresnel . . ." We laughed; we panicked; we changed every scene; we sighed; we prayed; we hugged good night.

I informed the cast an hour before they went on; they had no problem; the person who designed the lighting admitted he loved what we had done and had only two minor suggestions. I could not, and would not, have done it without Darla!

Eliza Doolittle

Success breeds success. Darla was asked to direct *My Fair Lady* for a well-known dinner theater in the area; she asked me to be Eliza; I accepted; the conflict began.

Darla was not going to announce the role of Eliza as pre-cast; from her point of view, it might keep someone from auditions whom she could use in another role.

To me, that was unethical. I said, "If you don't announce Eliza is pre-cast, I won't do the show." We battled; I won; we had a fabulous show with a fabulous cast.

New Venue: New Conflict

Success breeds success. Darla was asked to bring our production of *My Fair Lady* to a well-known theater in the area. Everyone was thrilled. The conflict began.

Neither the theater nor Darla was going to pay the expensive royalties. I believed that was unethical. "I won't do the show if we don't pay the royalties." We battled; we did not do the show; nobody won, but I would still make the same decision.

The Baby

I knew nothing about babies. Darla had two grown children. She had divorced, re- married, and gotten pregnant at 40-something. Neither Laura nor I had seen Darla since we moved to California. She and Dave brought their two-year-old "bundle of joy" to visit us for a few days. We were happy to see her and Dave; Jesse, however, was a handful, which I have come to understand is typical at that age.

Under Dave's influence, tutelage, and desire, Jesse was being raised very differently than Darla had raised her first two children, and very differently from how any of us had been raised. Taking twenty-five minutes to put on a pair of socks, while you are banging your head for ten minutes against the heating vent, getting your way at every turn with no resistance, and more, were all strange happenings to Laura and me, but having had no children, we just watched in awe.

Early one afternoon, Dave agreed to watch Jesse while Darla,

Laura, and I went to lunch to have an opportunity to talk and catch up without interruption. The conflict began slowly; it was my mistake; the consequence was unexpected, and it lasted a lifetime.

After discussing all our recent theater gigs, Darla asked me what I thought of Jesse. I worked my way around the question very nicely, while still being honest. We went on to other topics, and I was proud of myself for not sharing the whole truth. She came back again to Jesse and asked what I thought. It was getting hard; all my friends know, that if they ask me a question, I will give them my honest opinion, and if they do not want to hear what I truly believe, don't ask; surprising to Laura and me, I skirted the issue a second time; we moved on; I was relieved.

The third time is not always the charm. When she asked again, I said, "Do you really want to know?" She said, "Yes." I said, "He's a brat."

She never spoke to me again; my guilt, my sorrow, and my pain were unbearable; she died six years later of cancer without my having a chance to say goodbye.

Sometimes "the truth" hurts more people than just the person who hears it.

Your Thoughts:

#71 A Fantastic Lesson in Faith

He was a neighbor going through a rough divorce. I offered him our second bedroom. Laura didn't care as she was busy with her new career and had grown accustomed to my "taking in strays." Warren moved in.

Laura and I loved his Texas accent and cowboy ways. He was a fun addition to our lives. It was also a period of transition for me. I was not working at the time. I had been a sales manager for one of the many long-distance phone companies that popped up in the 1980s; it went the way of most of those businesses in the late 80s. Losing that job had been a trauma for me; I had never been released from a job before, and even though this was because the business closed, I still felt like I had been kicked in the stomach.

Since I moved to California, I had always decided which job I wanted and how long I stayed. I was at a loss now. I had been successful in sales, but I missed the rewards and the mental stimulation of teaching, I reconsidered going through the hoops to become a teacher, now in Orange County instead of Los Angeles, but there was still a lot of investment of time and money required for that option.

I was looking through the paper in the sales section of the classifieds again, when Laura said, "Here let me look through the paper and see what I can find." To be perfectly honest, I didn't think she would find anything that I would really like, but since I hadn't been successful, I was delighted that Laura offered.

She found a small little ad for a Learning Center Coordinator for a small private college, The Fashion Institute of Design and Merchandising (FIDM). The job was a tutor for the students. It was part-time and didn't pay much but was what I would enjoy.

I called and set an appointment for an interview. I will never forget walking into this very "artsy" Mercantile Building with a beautiful open lobby and balcony that followed the whole second floor around the building. I immediately felt excited about working there.

When I stepped up to the counter to indicate I was there for an interview, an instructor came up at the same time, with a grade book in hand, to pick up his messages. My whole body knew this is where I was supposed to be. My life was to be in the academic world in whatever capacity I could find. I knew at that moment I was, without question, supposed to be a part of this school.

They called me for a second interview and for a third. It all looked like I would get the job. Then I got the call; the woman who had had the position before had left the job because her son had been in a serious car accident and required her assistance for about nine months; he had recovered enough for her to return to work. Of course, they wanted her back, so I did not get the job; I understood intellectually, but not spiritually.

I was furious with God—as I understood God at that time in my life! Everything in my being *knew* I was supposed to be at that school, but it didn't happen. I felt betrayed. Why was I given that little whiff of what I love most just to have it taken away? If I hadn't felt with every fiber of my being that I was supposed to be there, I would have been fine, but I felt like *My SOUL* had led me there. I was confused and hurt.

Warren's mother was visiting us at the time; she was incredibly wise. She found a way to appeal to my ego, my sense of compassion, my spiritual foundation, and my mind, and she comforted me. She said, "Jeanne, you have lots of abilities (soothed my ego), the other person may not have the ability to take on any other job (aroused my compassion); God has something better in mind for you (stood me atop my spiritual foundation), and you will be able to go wherever He calls you (stimulated my imagination)." I thought a lot about what she said and found a way to be at peace with what had happened, even though the confusion lingered.

Three months later, in July, I received another call from FIDM; they needed a Psychology teacher; my bachelor's is in Psychology. Since they were a private college, they did not require all the hoops the state of California did to be an instructor. I accepted without hesitation and with tremendous joy.

I stayed with FIDM for eighteen wonderful years. My faith in THE SOUL (Spirit of Unconditional Love - "God" - the origin of all spirit, including *My SOUL*) was restored; I chose never to lose it again. My life as a teacher was restored; I chose to live it in gratitude. I was alive again!

#72 Class Acting Academy

Joy is a powerful motivator; it gives you the energy to build new dreams and go after them. I had always wanted to teach acting. Laura knew that. I mentioned to her that I would like to open my own acting studio; she was, as always, very supportive.

My teaching position at FIDM was part-time, so I had more time to pursue my dream. I named my business, *Class Acting Academy*. I rented a small space in a local strip mall, advertised a free four-hour acting workshop, *The Eight Axioms of Acting*, and built a wonderful student base. I offered classes for which the students would pay a fee. The fee was not exorbitant, which was great for the students, and it was enough to pay all my expenses and bring in a small profit, which was good for Laura and me.

The number of students grew, and I needed a larger space. One of my students owned horses and had a beautiful barn with a finished loft, which she said we could rent. She agreed on modifications we could make to accommodate our needs for the classes.

Warren was a good carpenter, and he helped construct the modifications. All was well, or so I thought, but I'm getting ahead of myself again. Before I continue with Warren, I need to take a detour.

One of the most significant changes in my life came from a lesson plan for the Scene Study Class I would be teaching. I was designing an acting exercise to help the actors ensure their characters were real and three-dimensional. The secret to that success lies in understanding why we feel what we feel and do what we do; if we can understand that, we can understand our characters in a way that will take us away from imitation or pretense and into authenticity. *My SOUL* gave me a formula - yes, a formula.

#73 P + B = E = A

Why do we feel what we feel and do what we do?

When we find the answer to the questions of why we feel what we feel and why we do what we do, then we can change how we feel and change what we do. That is what this formula—**P + B = E = A**—has done for me and hundreds of others with whom I have shared it.

The Meaning of the Elements of the Formula

P = Perceptions.	Our perceptions are our personal interpretations of people, places, and things. Our perceptions are our truths whether they are factual or not.
B = Beliefs.	Beliefs are what we have been taught by others, or what we have read, or seen, or experienced, or surmised, or deducted about the world, ourselves, relationships, and all other elements of

life, and we have accepted these beliefs as truth.

E = Emotions.   Emotions are feelings brought about by our perceptions and beliefs. Emotions are the fuel for our actions, but contrary to ordinary understanding, emotions DO NOT create, dictate, design, direct, or determine our actions!

A = Actions.   Actions are the physical expressions that result from our perceptions and beliefs. Actions ARE NOT a result of our emotions as most people believe.

Why two equal signs:

It is perceptions and beliefs that create both emotions and actions. Emotions come first in the formula since action requires fuel. Emotions are the fuel for actions, and that is all.

Have you ever felt apathetic? If yes, what did you do when you were apathetic? Most people answer: "Nothing." That is because apathy is the absence of emotion, so when apathetic, we have no fuel to perform an action.

Following is a made-up scenario to demonstrate how the formula works.

Scenario 1: Lunch with a Friend

I was sitting on a bench in the middle of the mall waiting for her - a friend of mine— Barbara. She is about 5'8" tall, with bright red hair, and walks with a lot of energy and purpose.

I finished a text I was sending; I looked up, and waaaaaay down on the other end of the mall—there she was, all 5'8" of her with her red hair flowing, her quick, long strides carrying her several feet at a time, heading straight my way, so I stood up, waved, and shouted, "Hey, Barb! Barb, here I am! Over here!"

And then, as everyone seemed to stop and stare, and the redhead ignored me, I realized, she was not Barb.

Oh my! I looked around sheepishly and perceived people laughing at me, believed I made a fool of myself, and—feeling embarrassed—I sat down and pretended to read an email!

Summary of the Scenario using the formula:

I look up from my emails, and I think I see Barbara at the other end of the mall. That is my **(P) perception** - my personal interpretation - <u>my truth</u>.

Because my **(B) beliefs** about Barbara are that she is a good friend whom I like and whose company I enjoy; I feel positive **(E) emotions**, which give me the energy to perform the **(A) actions** of standing up and yelling, "Hey, Barb. I'm over here."

I then **(P) perceive** that I am wrong, and since I **(B) believe** that I made a fool of myself, and I believe that making a fool of myself is a "bad" thing, I experience **(E)** shame and then **(A)** sit down and attempt to escape into my emails. I realize that my first perceptions were factually incorrect.

If I had believed that making a fool of myself was a "funny" thing, instead of a "bad" thing, I may laugh at myself along with some other folks who are watching me.

If I believed that others should mind their own business, I might confront them and say, "Mind your own business!"

How can I change if I want to?

We feel what we feel and do what we do because of what we perceive + what it is we believe about what it is we perceive!

Our feelings and our actions will change automatically with any genuine change in our perceptions and beliefs.

Following is a real-life scenario.

Scenario 2: Drawers

Laura had a habit of leaving drawers open, especially in the kitchen, but also in the bathroom and the den. Of course, I would manage to run into the open drawers. I would not be too happy with Laura. As I was closing the drawers, I would be thinking to myself - "How difficult is it really to close a drawer!"

So, one day, after running into an open drawer (I know - I know - I should be more aware, but . . .), I was standing in the kitchen talking aloud to Laura (who was at work), mumbling about closing the drawers.

I realized at that moment that I was not at peace or feeling joy or experiencing unconditional love. I wanted to change what I was feeling and what I was doing.

Lesson 21 of *A Course in Miracles Workbook* popped into my mind: "I am determined to see things differently." So, I decided to see things differently.

A choice came to my mind: Would I rather have the drawers closed all the time, and be without Laura, or have Laura in my life and have open drawers to contend with? Tears came to my eyes at the thought of not having Laura in my life.

I looked at the open drawer and said aloud, with sincerity as I closed it, in the kitchen, by myself, "Hi honey - thinking of you." I closed another drawer and smiled as I said, "I hope you are having a great day." I closed the last drawer that was open, and said, "I love you."

I went about the rest of my day with joy and peace and unconditional love exuding from every pore. It was a fabulous reminder of how much control I have over my life. What I feel and what I do will change automatically when I choose to see things differently.

PS: We have since installed drawers that close automatically. J

Summary:

Perceptions plus beliefs create emotions (some form of love or fear) and the emotions serve as the fuel to perform the actions; however, the actions are also a direct result of the perceptions and beliefs, not a result of the emotions. If I did not perceive the person to be Barbara, and if I did not believe in Barbara as I do, I would not experience joy, and I would not stand and wave to get her attention.

If I did not choose to see the open drawers differently, I would not have felt differently, and I would have continued with the same behavior. My feelings automatically changed, and my actions automatically changed when I chose to see the open drawers as a loving reminder of having Laura in my life instead of seeing the drawers as an annoyance.

Most of us have known someone with an anger problem, and many times those folks work at controlling the anger - they shove it down - then grit their teeth - they count to ten, and so on. Ultimately, they explode. That is because they are trying to change the emotion instead of what is causing the emotion. They would need to change their perceptions and beliefs about whatever they are afraid of to eliminate the anger rather than trying to control it. Remember, all anger comes from fear. They would need to identify the real fear; they would need to face that fear, and they would need to change their perceptions and beliefs about whatever is causing the fear.

VITAL CONCLUSION

If I want to change
what I feel and
what I do,

I MUST change
my perceptions
and beliefs!

All *permanent* change in our lives comes from a change in our perceptions
and beliefs!

Your Thoughts:

#74 Guilt: Part VI–Warren

Warren was not the first person we had taken in during times of trouble, but he was the last. I was aware of Warren's exploits. I knew he had seduced three women in the complex since moving in with us. He had attempted his tactics on me; I was not susceptible to his wily Texas "sweet-talkin'" ways, nor to what he had to offer.

What I didn't know was that Laura had been his fourth.

During the time Warren lived with us, things started to change in Laura's and my relationship. She was becoming distant; it seemed she was laughing and playing more with Warren than with me. I confronted her with my concerns and was handed nothing but denial, of course. I confronted Warren, but he made me feel that I was being stupid and paranoid. I became paranoid thinking I was becoming paranoid.

Warren talked Laura and me into buying a mobile home; he had been raised in them and was able to expound upon the benefits. Homeownership sounded wise, so Laura and I bought a mobile home. I thought it would be an opportunity for Laura and me to have a chance to be alone again. Warren moved with us.

Before I had come to know the truth, I was certain my relationship with Laura was on the rocks. I didn't understand it. I questioned everything; why do they both get up so early before going to work? Warren seized my vulnerability and suggested I move in with Rose whose husband had left her; it might be good for all of us he said. I was so confused, I almost did.

For the first time, I decided to sleep on the couch; that's when it happened!

I was lying there. I could not sleep. I was so distraught thinking of leaving Laura, and suddenly, there was an extremely powerful force that shoved me from my back so hard that I sat up on the couch and was nearly thrust onto the floor.

The Voice said firmly, "Warren must go; you must stay!"

I just sat there trying to process what had just happened. It was an actual shove that had moved me to sit up; I was looking around trying to figure it out, when I realized, of course, it would make more sense for Warren to leave than for me to leave. I could sleep in Warren's room until Laura and I figured out what to do.

I asked Warren to move out; he had no choice. He came back several days later asking to speak with me. He swore—on a Bible—nothing had happened between them.

I kept questioning: How could I keep sensing something was there when there was nothing there? But there was something there, in our home, under our roof; in our living room, in his bedroom; my foundation crumbled under me when Laura finally confessed the truth.

Guilt overwhelmed me, as always. I felt I had driven her away with my fits of anger. I felt I had allowed her into my world when she was too young. It was she who initiated and pursued our relationship, but maybe she wasn't gay. I had anticipated this possibility early in our relationship; curiosity is a powerful force, but not now, not after thirteen years. What now? Thoughts of suicide came flooding back! I was not strong enough to go on without Laura, not yet, not now, maybe never.

It was late at night; we were out of energy; out of words; out of tears; we were out of Pepsi. I was "addicted" to Pepsi. Laura left the house to go to the store; I left the house to be alone. I drove two blocks and parked in the dark in a deserted parking lot of the strip mall. I wondered what she would think when she came home and found the goodbye note. I had to let her go. I didn't want her to stay with me out of a sense of guilt or out of fear that I may do something drastic; she knew me; she knew it was possible.

She had said she was sorry; she wanted to stay; I could sense the doubts. She had confessed she wasn't sure a gay relationship was the "right" thing. Warren's fundamentalist influence was evident. Laura and I had struggled with the issue before, but had moved beyond it, or so I thought.

I sat in the parking lot; I don't know how long. I had more words to say, more tears to shed, more questions to ask. I went home. Laura had more words to say, more tears to shed, more questions to ask.

Nothing got resolved that night; it was Friday, December 27, 1991.

My Prayer

I prayed—not to save the relationship, but to know the truth. Should we be together? Is our relationship strong? I prayed—not for things to go as my heart ached for them to go, but to go as my spirit and Laura's spirit would benefit from the most. I prayed—not for my will, but for THE SOUL to make its will known to me.

Monday morning, December 30, I stared into the room where Warren had slept. Laura and I talked about who would be sleeping there now. I paced. Laura was meeting Warren, expecting something to happen in her meeting with him to tell her what she should do. Then . . .

My SOUL spoke. I listened. I wrote down every word.

Miracles

Miracles are hard to put into words and even harder for some people to believe. *My SOUL* said, "Friday night, turn on the radio at 11:00 pm. **Have Laura choose the station**. Between 11:00 and 11:30, your song will play; when it does, know without a doubt your relationship is blessed." I was baffled. Nothing like this had ever happened before.

Our song was "I Love You Just the Way You Are" by Billy Joel. It had come out 15 years before. I wrote the message down, then I tried to cheat. I had wanted truth, but I weakened. I added "Wind Beneath My Wings" and "I Will Survive" to increase the chance a song would play that was in the message. I knew it was wrong; I knew it wouldn't work; it was not part of the plan designed by *My SOUL*. I knew the difference between the voice of *My SOUL* and my voice. I did it anyway.

She came home from her meeting with Warren; I didn't ask. I showed her the message from *My SOUL*; I asked her if she would do it; she said yes.

Friday, 10:45 pm; I placed the radio on the dining room table; we sat on the couch. She put her arm around me, turned my face toward hers, looked me in the eyes, and said, "We don't have to do this. I love you. I could never love Warren the way I love you. I want to spend the rest of my life with you."

I couldn't believe it. She was saying everything I had hoped for. She loved me; she loved me more than Warren; she wanted to spend her life with me. We could start again; we would be stronger for it. The nightmare was over!

But it wasn't.

There were specific instructions from *My SOUL*. *My SOUL* had always been my friend; suddenly, it loomed as an enemy. What if we followed the instructions of *My SOUL* and our song didn't play? What if we didn't follow the instructions of *My SOUL*, would our relationship be blessed? It would be so easy just to go to bed.

I couldn't do it. I couldn't ignore *My SOUL*. I couldn't walk away. My heart sank. What were the chances that a 15-year-old song would play on a randomly selected radio station between 11:00 and 11:30 pm on Friday, January 3, 1992?

Like Abraham and Isaac, the time had come to put our relationship on the altar of faith. If our song didn't play, I would have to walk away from Laura. God came first, above all else, above Laura, above our relationship.

It was 10:58. I signaled for Laura to turn on the radio. She pleaded, "We don't have to do this, really. I don't want to turn the radio on. It doesn't matter. I want to spend the rest of my life with you."

I got up and turned the radio on, *but* the instructions were explicit; Laura was to select the station. "Laura, you have to select the station, not me." Then, I admitted, "And the only song *My SOUL* said would play would be our song, not the others. I added them myself." Laura had to know the truth. The whole truth: there could not be confusion; there could not be doubt. Waiting for the truth was frightening.

Laura didn't study the radio; she just found a station without static and sat down. I sat down; we waited. Song after song played; none were sung by Billy Joel. It was 11:20; I was crying; I was losing hope; I was clinging to Laura preparing to let her go.

I don't know what we were talking about at 11:23 when Laura put her hand up to silence me mid-sentence. "Don't go changin' to try and please me . . ."; it was 11:23, January 3, 1992.

Laura's Turn

The miracle didn't end there. God had something to say to Laura. The musical *Jesus Christ Super Star* has special meaning to Laura; we would sing the whole album during long drives.

Immediately following our song, *I Love You Just the Way You Are*, the radio station played, *I Don't Know How to Love Him*. Neither of us had ever heard that song on the radio before, nor have we since. It was not a coincidence that that song played immediately after our song. Laura knew it meant that she was to love her higher power in a way she had never loved before. We cried; we laughed; we hugged; we rejoiced. Our relationship was blessed. I was depressed.

#75 I Could Not Do It

It took me three tries to get off the couch - not because of bad knees or a bad back or a bad headache; it was because of a bad depression. Infidelity can do that to a person. I knew I had to get off the couch and do something—anything, so I slowly shuffled to the kitchen, opened the dishwasher, and picked up a glass to put it in the cupboard, but I just stood there staring at the glass. *I could not do it.* I could not put the glass on the shelf in the cupboard. I just stood there with the glass in my hand as if in a fog. Finally, I put the glass back in and closed the dishwasher, went back to the couch, and sank into a vortex of deep sorrow and confusion. Depression is sooooo debilitating.

Several days later, which seemed like several months—time is so warped in the realm of the physical world—like Salvador Dali's clocks—I found Marianne Williamson's book, *A Return to Love,* in my hands as if I had just woken up with it there.

It had been years since I had studied spiritual materials; I was too busy living life; what I had forgotten was that life without spiritual vigilance often becomes difficult.

In her book, Marianne discusses *A Course in Miracles.* I decided to read it. When it said that there are only two emotions, which I had been teaching in my Psychology classes since 1972, and when it talked about perceptions and beliefs, which was the essence of my formula, and when it talked about forgiveness in the way I had been taught by *My SOUL,* I knew I had found the path I was to follow.

I spent every spare moment of the next year and a half studying the text and doing the exercises in the workbook. I cannot ever put into words what this book did for me at the most critical time in my life, and what it still does for me now. I am enthralled with its spiritual principles and spend each day of my life trying to live them.

My heart needed healing. Laura and I were together, but I was like a fractured mannequin trying to find the spiritual cement needed to make me whole again. *A Course in Miracles* is so much more than that; it is a salve that not only heals; it eradicates all the scars. The introduction states:

> This course does not aim at teaching the meaning of love, for that is beyond what can be taught. It does aim, however, at removing the blocks to the awareness of love's presence, which is your natural inheritance.

I knew I was being introduced to something special. I stopped reading and allowed the echo of: "*love's presence* is my natural inheritance . . . love's presence is *my* natural inheritance . . . love's presence is my *natural* inheritance . . . love's presence is my natural *inheritance*, reverberate throughout my body, and I began to feel a healing vibration, which filled me with hope. The Introduction to *The Course* ends with:

Nothing real can be threatened.

Nothing unreal exists.

Herein lies the peace of God.

I felt tremendous power in those words: *Herein lies the peace of God.* That's what I wanted; that's what I needed, the peace of God, but what is real and what is unreal?

When I read the text again after completing the Workbook, I had a remarkable understanding of its intentions and a grand awareness of that which is real and that which is unreal, and in that understanding does indeed lie the peace of God.

Your Thoughts:

#76 Fear of Loss

All anger, frustration, impatience, and all other negative emotions come from fear. All fear comes from a sense of loss or scarcity. Fear comes from the belief that we have something that can be taken away or that there is something we want or need that we will not be able to attain. The object of our attention does not have to be physical. We may believe our integrity is being threatened, our control is being taken away, or we will be abandoned or denied our freedom.

The fear of losing Laura had blinded me. The miracle restored my sight. I can honestly say, I did not feel anger toward, or condemnation of, Warren or Laura; my spiritual foundation led me away from those feelings. "Forgiveness is not something we can do; it is the result of what we stop doing." I did not condemn, so forgiveness was not necessary.

However, there were real trust issues that arose and depression that I needed to deal with. There would be times I was convinced Laura was having another affair because it took her longer to get home than I thought it should, or I couldn't reach her by phone, or she wasn't where she said she would be. Those were difficult moments.

And there was deep depression. The betrayal was hard; I had thought that Laura's and my love was invincible, and I also did not expect to be betrayed by someone I had reached out to help, but Warren was a different person than I had thought.

Laura and I maintained honest communication. When I went through those times, I brought them to Laura; I never let them fester or get magnified. I never blamed Laura or Warren for my feelings; my feelings are my own responsibility, but Laura understood why the lack of trust and the depression were there. She was always extremely patient when I would tell her of my fear and lack of trust.

I never accused her; I never threw the situation in her face with condemnation; I always merely shared that I was feeling insecure and that I needed her help. She never chose to be a victim of my questions and doubt; she always remained patient, she would explain the circumstance without defensiveness, and she would provide the words and actions I needed to solidify our relationship once again. Laura is a miracle.

There is a magnificent ending to this story. Laura and I have now been together for forty-seven very happy years in 2025 (except for the little "bump" in the road). I did a lot of growing and so did Laura, and we are genuinely a wonderfully happy couple today. That "little bump" in the road became a fabulous blessing for us. All pain is gone, and all love lives on. Now I get off the couch and empty the dishwasher with ease and with joy. *We were officially married on June 17, 2008, in Southern California.*

Your Thoughts:

#77 What Unconditional Love Is Not: Part II

Some people believe that unconditional love is not achievable. Some people fear that, if they love unconditionally, they are then expected to accept, without restraint, whatever behavior someone demonstrates. Some people believe that unconditional love usurps reason. Some people believe that we must believe in a god to experience unconditional love.

I have three beliefs that help quell, for me, the concerns expressed above. The first two beliefs are rather obvious; the third belief is not. The first belief is that I live in many different worlds all at the same time. The second belief is that there is a universal law of Cause and Effect that functions flawlessly in the spiritual world. The third, and most important belief, is that the Law of Cause-and-Effect functions separately and independently from unconditional love.

The First Belief

I live in many different worlds all at the same time. I live in the physical world, the mental world, the emotional world, and the spiritual world, and it is in the spiritual world that unconditional love abides, and, if I choose to, I can access that world and incorporate that love into all of my other worlds.

The Second Belief

An important facet of the Law of Cause and Effect is that it does not punish! The law is objective. It has no bias, no prejudice, no agenda. It is a law that functions flawlessly in the spiritual world, and it is a law that is reflected (though not always flawlessly) in each of the other worlds in which I live.

In the physical world, if I stick my finger in a socket, I will get shocked. In the mental world, if I apply a flawed syllogism, I will end with a flawed conclusion. In the emotional world, if I am without faith I will experience fear, and in the spiritual world, what I sow, so shall I reap.

The Law of Cause and Effect does not punish. In the physical world, the socket does not create a shock to punish me for sticking my finger there; the shock is a natural consequence of the laws of physics. In the mental world, the flawed syllogism does not create a flawed conclusion to punish me; the flawed conclusion is merely a natural consequence of the laws of logic. In the emotional world, my faithlessness does not create fear to punish me; fear is a natural consequence of the lack of faith. In the spiritual world, the hatred I receive from any seeds of hatred that I may sow is not a punishment for sowing seeds of hatred; it is a natural consequence of the Law of Cause and Effect. Karma is not punishment, for Karma does not condemn.

The Law of Cause and Effect does not reward. Light is not a reward for turning on the switch; light is a natural consequence of the laws of physics. A syllogism does not reward me with a logical conclusion when I follow the rules of logic; the logical conclusion is a natural consequence of the laws of logic. Love is not a reward for the love I share; it is a natural consequence of cause and effect being the same thing. Karma is not a reward. The Law of Cause and Effect does not implement judgment of any sort; it merely functions flawlessly.

The Third Belief

If I apply the above insight to my social world, I see things differently than I did before. If someone commits a crime, then I can view the person's jail sentence as a natural social consequence of his socially inappropriate action rather than a form of condemnation of the person; going to jail is a natural consequence of committing a crime. If a society has agreed upon certain laws, then there need to be consequences when the laws are broken, but those consequences need not be, and hopefully are not, founded on, or drenched in emotion or retaliation or punishment. When I apply this concept, I can still love the person unconditionally, and at the same time understand and accept the natural consequences a person's actions create. The Law of Cause and Effect and Unconditional Love are to function separately from, and independently of, each other.

With this in mind then, I do not need to fear that, if I love unconditionally, I am then expected to accept, without restraint, whatever behavior someone demonstrates. Unconditional love does not usurp reason, unconditional love functions separately and independently from reason and justice.

#78 Avoiding the Sting

There is a way to avoid the sting of the Law of Cause and Effect. I can stick my finger in the socket and still escape the electric shock; I can use logic and avoid a flawed conclusion; I can live in the world and escape the fears that seem to permeate my life, and I can escape the pain of the poison fruit of which seeds I plant.

In the physical world, if I am grounded in the appropriate attire, I will be safe from the negative effects of the electric shock. Being grounded in the proper attire does not mean the shock will not occur; it means I will not feel the sting of the shock.

If I am grounded in the rules of logic, I will be safe from the sting of creating a logically flawed conclusion. Being grounded in the rules of logic does not mean that all conclusions will be true; it means they will be logical. Let me take a little detour.

A Little Detour - Syllogisms

1. The following is a correctly formulated syllogism: ***All dogs are***

animals. Lassie is a dog; therefore, Lassie is an animal. Not only is this syllogism correctly constructed, thus, providing a logically sound conclusion, but the syllogism also results in a factually true conclusion. However, that is not necessarily always the case.

2. The syllogism, ***All dogs are mean. Lassie is a dog; therefore, Lassie is mean***, is indeed an accurately constructed syllogism resulting in a legitimately logical conclusion, but the conclusion is not a true one. The Lassie many of us came to treasure in the television show featuring a very loving collie demonstrated not all dogs all mean. The false conclusion results from the false foundation of the syllogism above: "All dogs are mean." That is a false statement and leads to a false conclusion.

Back on Track

If I am grounded in faith—an unwavering trust - a "knowingness" without the possibility of doubt, I will experience an immeasurable sense of comfort, a feeling of security and safety. I will live without fear. Being grounded in faith does not mean that threatening things will not happen; it means I can preempt the sting of fear with tranquility.

A very key question is: what do I need to have faith in? I have come to have faith in the awareness that I am spirit; I am peace; I am unconditional love; I am joy; I am eternal; I am invulnerable; and that in this world of time, all things work together for my spiritual well-being.

If I am grounded in unconditional love, I will live in joy. Being grounded in unconditional love does not mean I can avoid drinking the poison of the unloving seeds I have sown in the past; it means I will accept the consequences of my actions with grace and dignity and peace.

Being grounded in unconditional love does not mean I will always be treated justly; it means I will see beyond injustice to the peace that "passeth" all understanding. Unconditional love reaches beyond reason, which allows events to flow through me with my full awareness of their purpose, not their pain.

If I choose to make it so, the spiritual world can permeate all my other worlds; it can become the only world in which I aspire to live consciously. It is the world in which I can live free of pain and suffering even as I continue to function well in all the other worlds. Each person's spiritual journey is a unique combination of his or her individual endeavors intertwined with others moving toward discovering, understanding, living, and "being" unconditional love.

My journey is individual. I make my own choices every day that either bring me closer to my spiritual destiny or take me further away. My journey is intertwined with others since it is others, as well as my "self," whom I am to love unconditionally.

Though I have faith there is a Spirit of Unconditional Love far greater than I can conceive, I do not hold as true that it is necessary to believe in a god to experience unconditional love. If I understand unconditional love is the result of a choice to see the world without condemnation, then I can understand that believing in a god is not a requirement to achieve peace. However, believing, or not believing in God has no impact on the truth of whether God exists. I believe I have met that entity - heart-to-heart!

What Unconditional Love Is Not

Unconditional love is not foolish.

Unconditional love is not blind.

Unconditional Love is not ignorant.

Unconditional love is not stupid.

Unconditional love is the result of seeing without condemnation.

But, before I can see without condemnation, I must discover what fears are blinding me.

Your Thoughts:

#79 Courage Personified

I couldn't stay with him another day. I just couldn't. I was disappointed in myself; I had hoped I could handle things better, but I couldn't.

It started with a phone call. It was Mom; she wasn't doing well; she never complained. I was on the next flight. Laura did not go. I did not get a substitute for my classes; I thought I would be gone for just the weekend.

Flying across the country was not as difficult then as it is now. There are some things that really were better in "the good old days." My brother picked me up at the airport and took me to mom and dad's house. Mother had lost a lot of weight and was very pale.

On the second day I was there, we took mom to the hospital. They admitted her. Dad and I stayed until visiting hours were over and came home. Around 2:00 am, Dad got a phone call; mom was not conscious; they were not sure if she was going to pass away or not, and Dad made one of the worst decisions of his life. Mom was dying. She had made it clear and had put it in writing, not to take any life-saving measures, but they had not taken the advanced directive with them to the hospital. They called dad; he told them to put her on life-support - a decision that could not be reversed easily.

He woke me up, and we went to the hospital. Mom was conscious when we got there, and she was furious! As usual, he had done it his way. As soon as it was a reasonable hour West Coast time, I let Laura know the situation. I called the school and let them know that I would be staying in Maryland, and they got my classes covered.

Mom was a survivor, so she grabbed onto the idea that she could go home with a portable ventilator, and that she could do okay that way. What they failed to tell her, but they had told dad, was how expensive that option would be. The whole way home he was depressed, distraught, and angry. Not because mother was dying; all he kept repeating was: "I'll lose everything. I'll lose the house. I'll lose everything. I don't know where I'll go. I won't do it. I'll commit suicide first. That's my only option—suicide." I listened to that all the way back to his house.

The next day, I asked the doctor if he had told my mother about the cost of her choice, and he said, "No." Dad then told them that it was her wish to not be on any life- support system. There were two problems: once the doctors put her on the ventilator, it was very difficult at that time to legally and ethically take anyone off. The second problem was they were not at all certain of dad's intentions. Mom had said to them when she was admitted - "Help me! Help me!" They read that as a cry for help for something other than for her medical care.

I stepped in. I knew mother would want to know the truth before going home with the portable ventilator; she had a right to the truth, and she would be upset to find out she had not been told everything. I asked the doctor to let me tell her. He trusted me.

I then embarked on the hardest thing I have ever done in my life. I told mom the whole situation: what it would mean if she went home with the vent, dad's fears, and other issues related to that decision. She listened quietly and then opened her arms to give me a hug—a rare moment. I left her bedside and sobbed.

I then arranged for all the doctors on her case, the social worker, and any other relevant personnel to meet with her, give her all the details of her circumstance, allow her to ask questions, and be informed of all the ramifications of each choice. I stood by her side through the whole meeting.

At that point, it had now been a week, and I could no longer stand to look at dad much less stay there another day with him. Had I known what was to happen next, I would have stayed with my brother instead of going back to California.

It was a Friday when I told mom I had to get back to my classes - that was the only excuse I could think of. She just said, "Do you think you can come back next Friday?" Mom never asked for anything, so I knew it was important to her that I come back, though I had no idea at that time the real reason she wanted me to return. I told her, "Of course, I'll come back," and I made those arrangements while at the airport waiting to go back to California.

What I did not know was the arrangement she had made with her doctor! She had asked him to take her off the vent; he had refused, but mother could be very persuasive. They made a deal; if she made that request of him three days in a row, he would follow her wishes. I went back on Friday, but it was for mother's funeral, and I knew then why she had asked me if I could return.

Dad knew. He knew all about the past and the present. He knew it all, which is why when he waved good-bye to me at the airport after mother's funeral, he said, with a knowing look, "Have a nice life."

Your Thoughts:

#80 Again and Again

My SOUL is so patient, so loving, so kind! The voice never gets frustrated, weary, impatient, or disgusted no matter how many times I miss the mark, always there waiting for me to begin the conversation and to invite Him in for a chat.

I was not at peace - of course. We cannot be at peace when we harbor anger, condemnation, hatred. That was me when I got back to California. Livid to the core! Laura was also patient, and when she heard of all the antics (and there were more), she too was not happy with my dad. Laura had never liked my dad.

However, I cannot go long without a chat with *My SOUL*. I needed to start again with how and why to forgive. I had to start from the beginning.

1. No one can make me angry - only I can do that. 2. Dad is not responsible for my feelings; I am. 3. Neither dad nor I are remembering the truth of who we are. I mean these words. They are not rote; they are deep and moving. All the lessons *My SOUL* shares go deep; that's why I return to them; they are real, and they bring peace.

After a day or two, I decided to be still and invite the voice into my life to provide guidance on how to eliminate the anger. I was willing! Nothing happens unless I am willing. I want to live in unconditional love no matter what the challenge.

Lesson 21 in *A Course in Miracles* says, "I am determined to see things differently."[29] Lesson 23 says, "I can escape the world I see by giving up attack thoughts."[30] Lesson 31 says, "I am not a victim of the world I see." I was now determined to see things differently, I wanted to give up my attack thoughts, and I wanted to experience the love I truly am, so I listened for the voice to tell me how.

I was reminded that all anger comes from fear and that I was to begin by determining what I was truly afraid of. That was going to take some time; however, "Fear not, Jeanne. Remember that I am with you always." was whispered in my ear. I gave myself several days to search deeply and honestly. The discovery was insightful.

The first thing I realized is that I was fighting his need to control everything, and I realized, too, that I was wanting to be in control of everything just as much. I wanted to control his behavior toward mom and me. I wanted to control the decisions that were made regarding mom, I wanted to control his anger and his condemnation, and the list went on.

Then I realized that I feared he would never see me for who I am. He always assumed I had a hidden agenda for everything, and that is the exact opposite of who I really am. I found out that he had never believed I had been raped; he believed I had gone to bed with one of Pam's fiancé's friends. One time, when he and mom visited our home, he pointed to a plant we had and said that he knew that was marijuana. I proved to him it was not, and I shared with him that I had never had an interest in drugs of any sort. But having hidden agendas, and even deceit, was a perfect reflection of how he was perceived by those who knew him best. In psychology, it's called projection.

I feared that forgiving him would justify his actions, when I was reminded again that, if I feel a need to forgive someone, I have first condemned him and his behavior rather than seeing him as a child of God and his actions as a call for love.

Anything not of love is of fear, and so I began to realize that dad must have lived in a lot of fear and how tragic that was. The compassion began to grow. I knew little of dad's life before I was born; I have no idea what challenges he faced. I began to think less about myself - I was going to be fine if I chose to be - and I began to see dad as someone who did not realize how much he was loved by a power so much greater than himself. If he had only known . . .

I used to call mom about every two weeks or so just to check in and hear her voice. When two weeks passed after her funeral, I was guided to call dad. That was not an easy request to fulfill! I had not yet resolved all my intensely negative feelings. My mantra is: "Do only that which you can do with love." That did not seem to fit, but I love *My SOUL*, and I know what is asked of me is always for my best.

Thank goodness Laura was there. I don't remember the details, but the conversation did not go well. It took everything in me to do it again two weeks later, but I was determined to conquer my fears and do the most loving thing I could which was to work on healing the relationship.

This went on for several months, and I began to see the conversations going in a different direction. I would choose to be still/quiet and listen to *My SOUL* before calling; I would feel peace, and I worked to keep that in my heart during the phone calls, realizing that I am the only one who can disturb my peace. The irony is, if I must work at being at peace, I am not at peace! I kept at it though, and things began to change.

I found I was resisting dad less, being reminded that we energize that which we resist. I found myself embracing his freedom to be and do and say anything he wanted to be and do and say. I was embracing his freedom to live his own journey without having to meet my expectations, and I found that the more freedom of his that I embraced, the more freedom I experienced. It was when I found myself genuinely laughing during one of our phone calls that I realized I had moved forward, but it did not take long to slip back when he was critical of me again and again and again.

I needed to remember that no one can define me but me; no matter how someone else may see me or how critical they may be of me, I am the only one who can define who I am. I am a child of God. I am love. I am joy. I am peace. No one can take that away from me. I became stronger.

About a year after mom died, I was ready to do the unthinkable; Laura would have to agree. She did. We invited dad to come for a visit. I wondered if I would be able to give him a hug.

He came; he was the same, but I was not, and I gave him a hug. Dad visited a couple more times before he passed away in 2002. By then, I had come to be grateful for him. He had become an important Buddha (teacher) in my life. He was the treadmill in my spiritual gymnasium. It is easy to love the loveable, but unconditional love muscles need to be exercised; they need a daily workout to stay strong and flexible so we can run past the ego's mask to the truth of who everyone is - a child of God - often lost in the forest of this illusion.

Dad eventually developed dementia. My brother and his wife Sue Ann took excellent care of him, first in their home, and then in a wonderful local facility. I visited once before Dad passed away. He was depressed when I visited; he had been an independent person all his life, and he did not like having to be taken care of.

I sat with him and listened, and then I said, "Dad, remember, as a Mason and a Shriner, you used to visit people in the hospital and bring them joy. You were always good at making them laugh." He said, "Yes." I said, "And do you remember how it used to make you feel." He said, "Yes, I felt like I was making a difference, and now I can't do that anymore." "But, Dad," I said, "if there had not been anyone for you to visit, you would have missed experiencing that joy of giving and sharing. You are now providing others the opportunity to experience that joy. The coin has two sides, you are now just the other side of the coin, but you are still playing a vital role in the lives of others." When he looked up, I saw tears in his deep blue eyes, and below them was a smile I had never seen before. He nodded and looked down. I gave him a hug and said my final goodbye.

Working through my condemnation of dad has proven to give me joy and freedom I could not have experienced otherwise. I had finally let go of the past. The past always clouds the now; I want to see clearly now. I love the song from *Godspell*:

Day-by-day. Day-by-day.

Oh, Dear Lord three things I pray.

To see thee more clearly;

Love thee more dearly;

Follow thee more nearly, day-by-day.

Your Thoughts:

_____

_____

_____

_____

_____

_____

_____

_____

_____

_____

_____

_____

_____

_____

_____

_____

#81 Another Move with Life-Changing Events

Laura and I stayed in the mobile home for about eleven years, then we wanted to get out from under the raises in rent for the property on which our mobile home sat.

In 2002, we moved into a fabulous apartment in Orange, California. During that time, two life-changing events occurred. On February 2, 2002; Laura and I received the official paperwork indicating that we were Domestic Partners in the State of California. That fact became extremely important legally the very next year, but there was more to happen in 2002 that changed our lives dramatically.

Dad died and since mom had passed away ten years earlier, my brother and I received an inheritance—it was a significant inheritance, at least the sum seemed significant to Laura and me; Laura and I could now afford to buy a home; if we acted wisely, we could own the home outright.

Angie, our former apartment manager and friend, had always talked about how she wished she could live in a place called Leisure World (now Laguna Woods Village); it was a community for senior citizens. The community had six clubhouses (now seven), four swimming pools, over 250 clubs, an internal bus system, groundskeeping, and many, many other wonderful amenities. A person had to be at least 55 years old to live there, unless they were the spouse of someone who was fifty-five or over, of course.

I qualified, so Laura and I investigated the community. We set up a couple of appointments with some realtors responsible for different properties, and we came to realize that there was one model that we liked the best, a *Seville*.

The next week, we saw an ad in the paper for a Seville, and an open house was scheduled for both Saturday and Sunday afternoons. We went Sunday afternoon, but no one was there. The next-door neighbor saw us and informed us that the owners had gotten two bids on Saturday, so they did not show up for the Sunday open house.

We were disappointed. The location was ideal, the model was the one we wanted, and very few of those models were available at the time; it was also another one of those, "This is meant to be" moments for me, so I decided not to lose faith this time.

The next week, we saw the same ad again; we wondered if the owners had merely forgotten to take the ad out of the paper; since we weren't sure, we decided to call.

The owner answered, and he informed us that both deals had fallen through. The home was being sold by the owner, so no realtors were involved; the owner said he would meet us at our earliest convenience; we went the next day. We walked in and fell in love with the home's wonderful natural light, the medium oak hardwood floors that matched our furniture perfectly, the built-in bookcases for all my books, the high ceilings, the loft on the second floor which overlooked the living room, the fresh paint and new carpeting throughout the rest of the home and so much more. We shook hands and bought the house that day with a 30-day escrow.

Two weeks later, the escrow company informed us that since Laura and I were not married, she would have to register as my caregiver or as a guest with none of the privileges of an owner, such as going to the pool without an escort.

I was livid! Laura was not going to live in this community under any false pretense or in any limited position, period. I called the escrow company and explained that we had the paperwork to prove that Laura and I were legally Domestic Partners and that we should be viewed as having the same privileges as a married couple.

We had proof of a joint bank account for over 20 years, and we would not accept anything less than being registered as a legal couple with all privileges awarded to Domestic Partners. We had never lived a lie, and we were not about to start now by saying she was a caregiver or guest. Then I asked if I needed to call the ACLU. I had never challenged such a circumstance by presenting a threat, but I was ready to go to the Supreme Court if necessary. Laura was never going to be treated like a second-class citizen in my lifetime!

The escrow owner said he would take care of it, and he did. We set a precedent, and other domestic partners, and now married gay couples, have moved into the community without incident. It is heaven here; neither Laura nor I would ever want to live anywhere else.

Despite the fabulous results, I learned a lesson about what not to do as well as what to do. Unconditional love does not mean we merely acquiesce whenever the world hands us something that is not equitable; however, I learned that it is important to approach circumstances with loving determination rather than fear and anger.

I was not coming from love; I was coming from fear. I could have accomplished the same goals without wrapping the presentation of my desires in anger. I did not like how I handled the situation even though I was thrilled with the results. I have since come to believe, I could have achieved the same results with love and understanding instead of attack. My ego took over instead of *My SOUL*; will I ever learn?

#82 The Medium

A neighbor of ours, Sharon, committed suicide. Sharon's lover, Pete, was struggling desperately over Sharon's choice. He and Sharon had lost many friends and family members because of their affair. Sharon and her husband were life-long friends with Pete and his wife before the romantic involvement occurred.

Sharon could no longer handle the guilt, nor the separation from Pete who had chosen to stay with his wife who, herself, had threatened to commit suicide if he left her. The ironies of life never cease.

I befriended Pete when no one else would. I did not judge him, condemn him, or blame him, so he found a refuge, and we became friends. He decided to go to a Medium to see if he could contact Sharon. He didn't believe in any of that, but he was desperate for answers; Sharon had not left a note for him.

He went and was amazed at the things the medium was telling him; things she could not have known; things she could not have guessed. He asked me if I would go to her and tell him my honest opinion of her psychic abilities. After the Ouija board incident, I honestly was a little reluctant, but I could not say no to Pete; he was desperate to know my opinion. I went.

She told me there was a young man behind me, and she proceeded to describe Michael to a tee; she told me others had shown up there with us that day, too, then she proceeded to describe them: mom was there, and my father was with her, along with another man my mother's age whom the medium said my mother was close to. There was no way the medium could have known about Mom's very first and, I believe, her deepest love in life.

My mother had been in love with a young man who had been killed in a car accident when they were in their early twenties. She had always loved him; apparently, he was there with her based on what the medium said, and she said dad was not too happy about it.

Then she started describing a short, slender woman with wild, curly hair who was jumping up and down insisting on getting the medium's attention. At first, I couldn't place her and kept asking the medium to go on to other things, but then the medium said, "This woman is not letting me go to anyone else until you acknowledge her. She is throwing her arms up in the air in complete disgust that you don't know who she is!" Then it hit me . . . Darla! Darla was there!

When I said, Darla? to the medium, she said, "Oh that must be who it is; she is shaking her head yes and jumping up and down, and she is saying she is sorry."

I stopped breathing. I asked, "She is saying <u>she</u> is sorry? Are you sure? Is she possibly saying that I should be saying I am sorry?"

"No," the medium said firmly. "She is saying she is sorry." And I burst into tears!

Your Thoughts:

#83 In Light of Illusion

Often my studies have led to the questions: What is real? What is unreal? Is this world made of substance or illusion? Is there really a world of spirit?

I have come to believe, as Buddhism, Hinduism, Taoism, and many other ancient and current (*A Course in Miracles* - Christ-based) philosophies propose, the temporal world is an illusion and the world of spiritual oneness is the real world. I believe we make our own "reality" and it can be as ugly as our greatest fear or as beautiful as our deepest love. The only thing truly real is that which is permanent, and nothing of the temporal world—nothing of the ego - is permanent - only divine love and all its qualities—peace, joy, beauty, wisdom, and oneness is permanent and thus real.

With beliefs such as that, events such as what I experienced with the Ouija board and the medium and apparent evidence of reincarnation cause me to meditate on their meaning and their purpose. I have come to believe that we have made talking with those who have passed over, abilities to see the future, and reincarnation integral parts of the temporal dream we have created to serve as instruments designed to awaken our awareness and to give us a grasp of eternal life.

If a belief in reincarnation helps us realize that we are eternal, the belief is a helpful stepping stone in coming to realize that we were never human at all but were merely an idea within an idea, a lucid dream within a lucid dream. If, however, the belief in reincarnation promotes the ego by causing us to believe we are special, separate, and unique (i.e., formerly the Queen of Sheba or Samson), then it works against guiding us to the eternal truth of the no-self versus the true Self—the ego versus the Spirit.

If an Ouija board can "predict" the future, then the present cannot be the present, it must be the past for the future to be made known in the now. Then what is the present but a hiccup in the temporal diaphragm? Unless, of course, being able to predict the future is part of the dream which we have made for ourselves. We can create any circumstance we choose in a dream, and that, I believe is what we have done. Reincarnation, speaking with spirits, predicting the future and so much more are indeed "truths" within the _untruth_, the dreams within a dream.

It is not my intention to deny the veracity of reincarnation, or a medium's ability to speak with those who have passed on, or to deny the ability for the future to be "seen"; it is merely my contention that Shakespeare embodied a spiritual truth in his character's words, "All the world's a stage, and all the men and women merely players . . ." A play has been written; we have auditioned and been cast, and we all play our roles perfectly; then the curtain comes down, and we all celebrate the elaborate production together, as one: of one Mind, of one joy, of one peace, of one freedom, of one spirit of unconditional love.

In light of our illusion, everything makes perfect sense, and as such, nothing elicits fear. We are invulnerable spirits; nothing can harm us; only our egos are subject to pain and destruction. Anytime we are feeling anything but perfect peace, our ego is in the middle of the moment. What we believe (or know) makes a quantitative and qualitative difference in the life we live.

Quantum physics seems to be providing a scientific and physics-based foundation for exploring the possibility that the physical world, as we seem to know it and experience it through our five senses, may not be what it seems. Many people have incorporated quantum physics into their life philosophy.

Another one of my favorite explanations of Quantum physics, however, is not in a textbook, or in a book written in this century, but is found in an autobiography, and not the autobiography of a scientist—not even Einstein, but of a Hindu religious leader— Paramhansa Yogananda. The book is *Autobiography of a Yogi*.

The book was published in 1946, and Paramhansa Yogananda was the right religious leader at the right historical time to put the knowledge of physics into an understandable, spiritual context.

His comments on quantum physics happen in "Chapter" 30 of his book, *The Law of Miracles*. I believe it is a must-read for anyone who is interested in understanding the connection between physics, miracles, spiritual truth, God, and humankind. I strongly recommend reading the whole book to fully grasp and experience the power of the information in "30s" concepts and anecdotes. The complete book is available online to read at no cost. The temporal world as an illusion is far from contemporary thought.

Paramhansa Yogananda was raised in the Hindu faith and built many bridges during his lifetime between Hinduism, Christianity, Judaism, and Spirituality. It is important to know that the basic religious texts for the Hindus are the Vedic scriptures. They are ancient texts with knowledge and understanding that far surpasses what we seem to know and understand today. In those sacred texts, the word *"Maya"* translates into "illusion," and more specifically, an illusion of dualism and relativity perceived as the reality of man's world.

Paramhansa Yogananda explains *"Maya"* more thoroughly in the following excerpts from "30" in his autobiography.

> The ancient Vedic scriptures declare that the physical world operates under one fundamental law of *maya*, the principle of relativity and duality. God, the Sole Life, is an Absolute Unity; He cannot appear as the separate and diverse manifestations of a creation except under a false and unreal veil. That cosmic illusion is *maya*.

Every great scientific discovery of modern times has served as a confirmation of this simple pronouncement of the rishis ("illumined sages"— authors of Vedic scriptures). [30]

To surmount *maya* was the task assigned to the human race by the millennial prophets. To rise above the duality of creation and perceive the unity of the Creator was conceived of as man's highest goal. Those who cling to the cosmic illusion must accept its essential law of polarity: flow and ebb, birth and death. This cyclic pattern assumes a certain anguishing monotony, after man has gone through a few thousand human births; he begins to cast a hopeful eye beyond the compulsions of *maya*.

"The stream of knowledge," Sir James Jeans writes in *The Mysterious Universe*, is heading towards a non-mechanical reality; the universe begins to look more like a great thought than like a great machine."

From science, then, if it must be so, let man learn the philosophic truth that there is no material universe; its warp and woof is *maya*, illusion. Its mirages of reality all break down under analysis. [31]

Another great work of Hindu thought is the *Bhagavad Gita*, which portrays our internal struggle between ego and spirit as being played out on a battlefield. It is a powerful piece that leads us to the understanding that we make our own reality; we design our own experiences.

And then there is the Buddhist Diamond Sutra, written centuries ago and taught by Buddha himself. A fabulous revelation of what is truly real and what is not. The segment below is but a whiff of the feast offered in the Diamond Sutra.

Diamond Sutra - 3.

> All living beings, whether born from eggs, from the womb, from moisture, or spontaneously; whether they have form or do not have form; whether they are aware or unaware, whether they are not aware or not unaware, all living beings will eventually be led by me to the final Nirvana, the final ending of the cycle of birth and death. And when this unfathomable, infinite number of living beings have all been liberated, in truth, not even a single being has actually been liberated.
>
> Why . . .? Because if a disciple still clings to the arbitrary illusions of form or phenomena such as an ego, a personality, a self, a separate person, or a universal self existing eternally, then that person is not an authentic disciple." [32]

Jesus knew the secret of the illusion, which is why he was able to break the apparent laws of physics. His awareness of this temporal world being an illusion was the foundation for his peace, his joy, and his miracles. This secret is revealed in many of the writings left out of the current Bible and those texts are worth exploring.

I am bringing these great works of wisdom into this book because they, along with, *A Course in Miracles*, have brought me to an understanding of what is meant by this world being an illusion, and in light of that awareness, I see the world differently. If I am to experience the world with unconditional love, then I must change my beliefs and my perceptions. That does not mean I make up a new paradigm; it means I find the paradigm that reflects the truth of who I am as I have come to know myself from the inside out instead of from the outside in.

"Nothing real can be threatened. Nothing unreal exists. Herein lies the peace of God." [33]

Our egos panic at the thought; our spirits soar at the awareness of that truth.

#84 Knowing the Ending

It was not until I understood the words "this world is an illusion," that I experienced real freedom, real unconditional love, real peace, and real joy.

I have learned an important key to peace and unconditional love, is to recognize each event in our temporal lives, past, present, or future, is a "tabula rasa"—a blank slate upon which we write our own messages.

No message we write is ever neutral, though the slate upon which we write it is. No reaction to each message we write is ever neutral—our response is always one of love or fear, peace or war, unity or separation. The everlasting beauty is - we get to choose.

I went to see the movie *The Piano*. The story of the movie takes place in a rather isolated part of New Zealand during the late 1800s. It was a time in which men could buy wives. Alistair and George are the two main male characters.

Alistair literally has a wife "shipped" in. Ada arrives with a daughter and a piano. The piano is vital to Ada. At age six, she chose not to speak. Consequently, her vocal cords lost their strength, and so she could not speak. The piano is her greatest connection to the world.

Alistair does not understand the value of the piano to Ada, so he just leaves it on the shore. Damp salty air will destroy a piano. George does realize Ada's need and offers to trade some valuable land with Alistair for the piano and for free piano lessons.

A romantic relationship ensues between Ada and George. Alistair finds out and takes Ada to the backyard, places her hand on a tree stump, takes an ax, and goes whack! He cuts off two joints of her right index finger so she can no longer play the piano. I literally got sick to my stomach, distraught, and downright angry.

Alistair has Ada's daughter deliver the partial finger to George. George decides to leave New Zealand; he loves Ada and does not want to cause her any more harm.

However, Alistair's violent act is a turning point in everyone's life. He had intended to kill George, too, but comes to realize that he has been wrong about everything. He tells George to take Ada, the daughter, and the piano away with him.

The final scene has Ada sporting a prosthetic fingertip. We find out she is teaching piano and has also decided to learn how to speak again.

The Piano is certainly not a movie I would go to see a second time, but a friend wanted to see it; she did not want to go alone, so after an hour of persuasion, I went. I certainly did not look forward to the backyard, so I was shocked at my reaction. When the ax went whack, I made a motion of celebration and said "Yes!" aloud.

My friend looked at me as if I were crazy, of course. "What are you doing?" she whispered. I just smiled. I was celebrating over that incident because I knew the ending. I realized that Alistair's horrendous act had been the catalyst for creating the happy ending.

I realized, since I knew the ending, I perceived the "horrific" event very differently; I now saw the event as a "blessing" that created a major change in Ada's destiny, and because my perceptions and beliefs about that moment had changed, my emotions and actions changed.

I realized that I had written my own message on the same event each time I witnessed it and that the messages I wrote were quite different from each other. I got it; I finally got it. We cannot evaluate whether something is good or bad unless we know the ending.

I experience it over and over every football season; the fumble seems like a horrible thing until we intercept the resulting pass by the opponent and run it in for a touchdown. We celebrate the touchdown until the kickoff is blocked, and the other team scores, runs it in, and wins the game. We cannot assess the "good" or "bad" of any event until we know the final "score."

Spiritually, I now believe I know the ending, and it is a wonderful one for everyone.

We are spirit; we are invulnerable; we are eternal; we are infinite; we are of one Mind; we are unending unconditional love; we are imperturbable peace; we are unbound joy; we are limitless freedom; we are one with THE SOUL. And when I say, "we," I mean every single imagined person who ever has, does now, or ever will "exist" in this lucid dream.

There can be no exceptions, for we are one. If we exclude anyone, we exclude ourselves from experiencing the miraculous joy of the truth.

I have come to believe that every event in everyone's life, no matter how tragic it may appear on the surface can be used for our spiritual growth. All spiritual growth is on our understanding of unconditional love. Now that I truly believe that all things work together for my spiritual well-being, then all events, regardless of my initial reactions to the perceived difficulties in my life, are contributing to the happy ending that is my spiritual destiny.

Since I know the happy spiritual ending in store for all of us, I really have absolutely nothing to fear for myself or for anyone else.

Your Thoughts:

#85 San Francisco: A Wonderful Wedding

I thought of it on Tuesday, and mentioned it to Laura on Wednesday; we flew to San Francisco on Thursday, stood in line, in the rain and mist from 6:30 in the morning until 5:00 in the afternoon, winding our way around and into the City Hall on February 20, 2004. We were 22 people away from getting married when they closed the doors for the weekend, but we were given specific times to return on Monday—our time was 9:30. It was perfect.

I am not normally a spontaneous person, and Laura and I have never been activists for the gay rights movement; we just always live our lives in a quiet open way in the very normal worlds in which we found ourselves. Everyone in our personal and professional lives has always known of our relationship, and we never experienced any blatant prejudice, so we never felt a desire or need to march for our rights. We have never sought gay clubs or activities or places to hang out because we have always felt accepted wherever we were. However, we are, and always will be, enormously grateful for all those who have been activists; without them, we would not be as far along on the path of acceptance as we are.

So, this thought to go to San Francisco when Mayor Gavin Newsom announced that he was going to allow gay marriage, actually came out of the blue, and it was one of the most beautiful times in our lives.

We had some friends living in San Francisco, so we were spending the weekend with them. They picked us up at the airport on Thursday night, and they got up early with us on Friday morning to go stand in line.

The experience was one of unconditional love all day. Everyone in line was celebrating with and for each other, but what was so unexpected was how many other folks helped us celebrate that day. Car after car would go by with people honking their horns and waving and giving the thumbs-up sign. Suddenly, strangers would come up and hand us flowers, flowers that came from all over the country. People had gone to their local flower shops, bought flowers, and sent them to be delivered to those of us in line. Laura and I received flowers from people in South Carolina; they left their names on the card. We tracked them down and wrote to thank them for their kindness.

Everyone was taking pictures and sharing phone numbers; we were one. Even when some protesters showed up, we treated them with loving kindness, understanding their fears, and honoring their positions and their beliefs; we chose to give them the love that we hoped they would be able to give us one day. It truly was giving unto them that which we would like them to give unto us and treating them with respect and with the freedom for them to have their beliefs and live their lives as they chose as we hoped they would give us one day. The love was palpable and unconditional.

It turned out well that we got in as far as we did that day and that the decision to assign times for marriage ceremonies was made rather than having to come back on Saturday and stand in line again. Laura and I had the whole weekend to spend with our friends being escorted around San Francisco.

On February 23, Laura, Jack, Brad, Laura, and I went to City Hall. What a magnificent building. We hoped we would be able to stand at the very top of the gorgeous winding stairs, and we got the exact spot we wanted! Couples were getting married everywhere you looked; what a beautiful sight. We laughed; we cried; we loved.

When we returned from San Francisco, we came home to more flowers and cards and phone calls of congratulations. When I went to

FIDM the next day, they had a wedding cake for me to share with them and Laura. Love was in the air, and it was exhilarating to breathe.

Laura experienced similar sharing when she returned to work. What we already had known was confirmed; we were not just tolerated as a gay couple; we were truly loved and respected. We had been together for twenty-six years, it seemed like new.

We knew when we received our wedding certificates that they were not legal, so when they were negated later, it was no surprise nor was it disappointing for Laura or me, though many of our friends were outraged. We knew someday that there would be a moment when we could get married legally, though none of us ever thought it would come as quickly as it did.

June 17, 2008, just a little beyond our 30-year mark, Laura and I stood in a very, tiny room in the County Clerk's office in Laguna Hills, California, and took our vows for real and forever. We were surrounded by wonderful friends and strangers, other gay couples anxious to make their relationship legal in the eyes of the world, joyful to finally experience what many had dreamed of for so long.

The next day, Tuesday, June 18, 2004, there we were, in living color, on the front page of the very conservative Orange County Register—Laura and I took our vows. Why we were chosen I'll never know. The reporter also interviewed me, and I was on the Internet on the Orange County Register website. I wrote in requesting a copy of the interview and a copy of one of the pictures they had taken, so we have those wonderful mementos. *Love is a beautiful thing to live.*

Your Thoughts:

#86 What Unconditional Love Is Not: Part III

Unconditional love is not hard; it is natural. What is hard is letting go of our ego; once we do that; unconditional love is all we are. Letting go of the ego is letting go of our attachments, our attacks, and our fears.

Unconditional love is not something we do; it is "the experiencing of" what we are. We do not "do" happy; happiness is "the experiencing of" the moment. Happiness is the result of what we perceive and believe. Then, truth reaches beyond perception and into experience. Unconditional love is not outside the moment; it is the moment.

Unconditional love is not static. It must extend in order to be itself; love cannot contain itself; it must share. We are always extending who we are into the now, so we are either extending ego, or we are extending spirit.

We will always experience what we extend, so we are always experiencing either ego or spirit. Spirit will experience peace, joy, freedom, oneness, and unconditional love because that is what spirit is; ego will experience conflict, limitation, separateness, fear, anger, frustration, and conditional love because that is what ego is.

Unconditional love is not an exception to the formula: $P + B = E = A$ (pg.140). Our perceptions and beliefs about ourselves and others are what create our experiences. When we discover our true identity is spirit, we begin to live it, then we come to know it, then we come to be it. Then we can be in the temporal world, enjoy it, participate in it, and yet not be of it. To experience unconditional love, we embrace a path that shows us who we truly are.

There are infinite signposts directing us to those paths, and they all lead <u>inward</u>.

#87 A Zen Parable's Magnificent Wisdom

It is not our destiny we should place in God's hands; it is our peace. –Jeanne Sanner

Parables are wonderful ways to communicate. Well-written parables can touch nearly everyone in some way, and sometimes they can touch many people on several levels at once. Well-written parables reach deep into our souls and touch the truth. If we let them, they can tear down walls built over many years from many fears and attachments. The Zen parable "*Ah, so*" demolished such a wall for me.

Ah, so

The Zen master Hakuin was praised by his neighbors as one living a pure life.

A beautiful Japanese girl whose parents owned a food store lived near him.

Suddenly, without any warning, her parents discovered she was with child.

This made her parents angry. She would not confess who the man was, but after much harassment at last named Hakuin.

In great anger, the parents went to the master and charged him.

"Ah, so?" was all he would say.

After the child was born, it was brought to Hakuin. By this time he had lost his reputation, which did not trouble him, but he took very good care of the child. He obtained milk from his neighbors and everything else the little one needed.

A year later the girl-mother could stand it no longer. She told her parents the truth— that the real father of the child was a young man who worked in the fish market.

The mother and father of the girl at once went to Hakuin to ask his forgiveness, to apologize at length, and to get the child back again.

Hakuin was willing. In yielding the child, all he said was, "Ah, so." [34]

I used to experience anger and frustration over perceived injustices (and I still do at times—change is not always easy). Things that I saw as unfair riled my "rebel" and stirred my emotions into action with undaunted determination to "fix" the inequity.

I do not believe that it is morally wrong to be outraged by injustice; however, I believe I was spiritually unaware or naïve about my options; the parable "*Ah, so*" showed me a much more loving, peaceful, spiritually-sound option to injustice: *non-attachment.*

"Non-attachment" is not the same as "detachment." In fact, spiritually, I would consider them opposites. Detachment means deliberate separation, a desire to be apart from rather than a part of. Non-attachment means love without demands; dedication without desire; caring without constraints; involvement without expectations; in other words, it means a positive interaction without strings that tie the relationship into knots.

Non-attachment teaches how to care and not care at the same time. It means caring about the process but not the results; it means caring deeply about the now and not the not-now; it means living without fear, living joyfully with what life brings without concern about the consequences.

In the parable *Ah, so*, the Zen Buddhist Master beautifully demonstrates non- attachment. He shows non-attachment to his reputation, to the need for truth, to the need for justice, and most importantly he shows non-attachment to the child, which is the essence of the lesson I learned.

My first reaction to this parable was outrage. The injustice of it all! His reputation is lost; people choose to believe a pregnant young girl over the evidence of the Zen Master's "pure life"; he is given the responsibility of raising a child whom he did not father, and then . . . .**and then. . . .and then**, he is expected to just give the baby back regardless of his "attachment" to the child. No! No! No!

A short while before I read this parable for the first time, I was studying Lesson 23, *A Course in Miracles* Workbook, "I can escape from the world I see by giving up attack thoughts." To study this lesson and make it relevant to me personally, I made a list of the things I tended to attack at the time, and "injustice" topped the list. (The rest of the list included: stupidity, abuse, competition, resistance, self, and selfishness, in that order.) The lesson was teaching me that I should relinquish attack, but it did not teach me how; that's what reading *Ah, so* did; it showed me what non-attack looks like through the eyes of non-attachment.

Hakuin did not attack or fight the grandparents of the child when they came to him; he knew his words would mean nothing to the enraged grandparents who would believe their daughter under any circumstances.

He accepted without regret, or resistance, or retaliation, the circumstances the turbulent stream of life washed upon his shore. His non-attachment to the "meaning-less" slings and arrows of life, as he saw them to be, allowed him to move on in peace and joy to the "meaning-full" mission now facing him—caring for the child.

The part of the story in which I became most enraged was when the grandparents figured that their apology would be enough to heal the wounds of a damaged reputation. And then . . . **and then** . . . **and then** expect that it was perfectly okay to just take the child away without regard to Hakuin's probable "attachment" to the child, and the child's attachment to Hakuin; I fumed over this story for days, until I realized that my outrage was not constructive. Had I been in Hakuin's place, my rage would have caused me to attack, which would have only exacerbated the problems; it would have created resentment, separation, fear, frustration, and probably un-loving acts of retaliation by spreading the truth to preserve my reputation without regard to the pain it might cause the family. I also realized that Hakuin could accept the request for forgiveness without difficulty since he had not judged or condemned them; without condemnation, forgiveness is not necessary, but through non-attachment, there was no need to attack.

The injustices were irrelevant; Hakuin was impervious to the worldly consequences and lived in the moment of spiritual truth; a baby needed care and unconditional love, and so he joyfully provided those comforts to the child unexpectedly laid at his feet, and then chose to be joyful over the reunion of the child with its rightful family. His non-attachment made it such that the circumstance was never about him; it did not have to be about him since nothing external could disturb his inner peace.

I admire the Master's ability to accept the circumstance without a ripple of dread. He demonstrated the beauty of non-attachment and its natural extension, non-attack.

Non-attachment is a pathway to peace. It is the truth and the life and the way within each of us; we need only seek to bring it to the surface of our own awareness.

Christ consciousness was intended to be the core of Christianity, but the man named Jesus, who exemplified the Christ consciousness, as others before him had, such as Siddhartha Guatama, Lao-tzu, and others, has sometimes become the focus instead of the message of oneness and unconditional love.

I cherish this parable for the life-changing message it gave to me.

Your Thoughts:

_____

_____

_____

_____

_____

_____

_____

_____

_____

_____

_____

_____

_____

_____

_____

_____

_____

_____

#88 Guilt: VII–Final Resolution

The universe had one more lesson in guilt for me to experience before I would discover the final and most important element needed to eliminate guilt forever.

I was in a position of leadership of a group, and I had to inform someone that he could not be a part of the team anymore. Larry was very hurt and angry. He has chosen not to speak to me ever again. I struggled deeply over the incident; I had not handled it well at all.

At first, I thought the decision I made was right for me and for the organization, but now I do not believe that at all. I came from fear instead of love from beginning to end. The decision and the process were done in a hurtful way instead of a loving way. I believe Larry would have reacted the same way regardless of how I shared my decision with him, but I felt like a hypocrite—I spend much of my life talking about and trying to live love—unconditional love—compassionate love, and I had failed to achieve that during this unfortunate event.

As I struggled with the loss of a friend and with the self-chastisement for my decision and for the way I had handled the situation, another friend came to my rescue, *My SOUL*. The ever-consoling, wise, comforter simply began by saying, "Freedom." "Freedom," I repeated out loud, alone in my living room. "Freedom," the voice repeated.

It took me a little while, there were lots of applications of that word, but then, I realized what *My SOUL* was saying to me. "Of course: Freedom!" I jumped up and spoke aloud again. "How could I be so slow to get this?"

The ultimate experience of unconditional love lies in freedom! Unconditional love is the result of unconditionally, completely, totally, joyfully, embracing everyone's freedom, inside our illusion of time and space, to be who and where and how and why and what we are! Unconditional love is the result of embracing everyone's freedom to be separate—their freedom to reject—their freedom to attack—their freedom to love—their freedom to forgive— their freedom from and freedom to—their freedom from judging or being judged - freedom to be or not to be—complete freedom to exist in any form at any time in any place—infinite freedom—freedom without conditions other than our oneness; we can never change the truth of our oneness—embracing everyone else's freedom is the key to experiencing our own freedom.

We can experience only that which we give. When I embrace someone else's freedom, I grant myself the same. I build my own prison, bar by bar, as I construct a jail of "shoulds," "musts," expectations, assumptions, rules, and control over others—the guard on duty is confined within the prison walls as much as the prisoner.

Guilt does not want to grant freedom! Guilt is tenacious in its desire to have things be different from the truth. Guilt wants to go back and fix the situation or fix the other person or fix us—it wants to change the present by changing the past. We can only change the present in the present.

I was suffering over my situation because I was not embracing Larry's freedom to choose to be separate, to choose to reject me, to choose to condemn me. Once I accepted his freedom, once I totally accepted the way things were without a need to change anything or anyone in the situation, my guilt was released. I did decide to find ways to change myself in the present so that I would handle future events in a more loving way.

My life experiences with guilt have taught me many things. Guilt is always of the ego even though it may seem as if it is our love of someone we believe we have hurt that is the cause of the guilt. There seems to be an endless list of reasons to feel guilty: believing we've hurt someone by attacking them emotionally, physically, psychologically, or by neglecting them, rejecting them, betraying a trust, disappointing them, breaking a personal/social code, getting/having something "you don't deserve," being happy when you think you "shouldn't be," and on Infinitum. To change our emotions and our actions, we must change our perceptions and beliefs. (See #73.)

In reality—spiritual reality—we cannot hurt anyone, and no one can hurt us. It is only our ego-selves (which is responsible for our physical bodies, our negative emotions, our attachments, and all other elements of the physical world), that can be hurt. That does not mean we should not be sensitive to someone's ego, or even our own, but it does mean that we can relinquish the fear that whatever "damage" we think we may have caused is never permanent, even if it seems as if it were in this realm of time and space. Nothing in the temporal world is permanent.

What I have come to believe is that if we are to truly experience peace, joy, freedom, and unconditional love, we must constantly go back to the question: who are we really? If we really believe that we are eternal, infinite, invulnerable loving spirits, then we will come to know that nothing in this lucid dream can anyone's true identity—spirit - it is only the ego-self that is vulnerable to pain and suffering.

#89 Guilt–Part VIII: Conquering Guilt

Guilt is tenacious, and it needs attention. My experiences have taught me specific steps I can take to eliminate guilt, but those steps require a change in perceptions and beliefs if they are to be effective.

BE STILL and know that I am loved. It is in my stillness, in my desire to listen to the voice within, instead of the noise without, that I come to know the depth of the love that swaddles me.

Take ownership of my actions. All non-loving action is of the ego. It is important for me to acknowledge and accept responsibility for those moments I have acted out of fear instead of love.

Ask for forgiveness if I have acted unkindly. For many years I had wished my father had asked me for forgiveness; however, I learned that my forgiveness of others is not at all dependent upon them; it is I who must relinquish my condemnation of them and their actions if I am to experience the beautiful freedom forgiveness brings. However, in my asking for forgiveness from others, I am acknowledging my mistake and letting the other person know that I have learned something from the situation.

Let go of my fear of the future. Some guilt comes from my imaginings about what the future would have been like had I done, or avoided doing, something, and I tend to imagine that the future would be better had I not done what I did or if I had done something different. I want to live in the now with unconditional love and the future will take care of itself.

Relinquish self-condemnation by recognizing the only thing I can change is me in the present. Learn from the event and apply the lesson of unconditional love to my life from this moment on, including loving myself unconditionally. If I choose to change myself in ways that will reflect the love that I am, then I have made the best of the situation, and I can move forward. Getting stuck in the past does not make the present or the future a better place for anyone.

Embrace the "victim's" freedom to be who, what, where, and how they are.

Embrace acceptance (ego analyzes; Holy Spirit accepts).

Embrace joy. My guilt will not have a positive effect on the world, but my joy can. I am joy; it is important that I be true to myself and embrace the joy that I am. Staying in guilt does not allow me to be true to myself.

The only effective remedy for my guilt is the Salve and the Shield. Freedom from condemnation is the salve that loosens the barnacles clinging to my vessel; faith is the shield that prevents them from adhering to me again. The salve and the shield are more powerful than the ego. Ultimately, I have come to learn that guilt is a terribly destructive force born of the ego that corrodes my present and my future.

There is one other step. I want to be grateful. If I really believe that all things work together for my spiritual well-being, then I will come to a point at which I am grateful for every experience in my life. I will come to examine each event for the nugget of unconditional love that lies at the core of all of my imaginings, and when I grab onto that nugget, I will experience all that I am.

Gratitude is one of the most powerful experiences a person can have. An attitude of gratitude fills me so full of joy there is no room for anything else.

We can conquer guilt, and I sincerely believe it is important that we do.

Your Thoughts:

#90 What My Smiley-Face Mug Taught Me

I have a smiley face mug. It's my favorite mug for the very reason that it is always smiling.

My mug sits on my computer table. I was rolling my computer table from the living room to the den to do some printing (I didn't have a wireless printer at the time). I had reached the dining room when my favorite mug fell off the computer table and onto the hardwood floor. When I looked down, I was genuinely sad to see that the handle of my favorite mug had broken into several irreparable pieces.

I just stood there for a minute, looking down at my wounded companion, staring at the scattered handle chips, assessing the damage, and mourning the loss.

My eyes slowly moved from the chips to the cup portion of the mug lying next to the dining room table leg. There it was, fully intact, in all its glory, smiling up at me just as happy as ever. I suddenly realized, nothing, absolutely nothing could daunt its spirit; I shook my head in admiration and smiled back.

I started picking up the pieces, gently, and with regret; I threw the shattered remains of the handle into the kitchen trashcan and started to do the same with the cup while silently saying goodbye to my friend, but I could not bring myself to put that smiley face in the trash. I just could not do it!

So, today my mug still smiles at me from my computer table, only now, instead of being filled to the brim with coffee, it is filled beyond its brim with lots of colorful pens and pencils; it could not be happier, and neither can I. It is not what happens to us that matters, it is how we handle what happens to us that determines the quality of our lives.

#91 Loving Kindness

There is a huge potential pitfall in the philosophy I have developed for myself. As with any belief, there is always the possibility of misuse or abuse, and mine is no exception.

I believe my true identity is spirit. As spirit, I am invulnerable. I believe the true identity of all the brothers and sisters whom I think I see are also spirit; in fact, I believe we are one spirit; one Mind that has imagined this temporal world; just as one author imagines many characters in a single play.

As spirit, all the brothers and sisters I think I experience are also actually spirit and are, thus, invulnerable. No one is a victim—ever!

I believe we make our own reality in this illusion of time and space. We do that by bringing to ourselves events that will awaken us to our spiritual truth if we choose to read the signpost each event places in front of us.

We also make our own reality by writing on each event our own interpretation, our own emotional, psychological, and physical experience based totally on our current beliefs about what it is we think we perceive and what it is we believe we are.

In other words, I believe I am totally responsible for everything that happens to me. I bring into my sphere the events needed for me to find my spiritual truth, and I am totally responsible for what I do with, how I react to, how I interpret, and how I apply the lessons from everything that happens to me.

No one can make me angry; no one can make me sad; no one can hurt my feelings; no one can impact my life in any way other than what I choose. The more power I relinquish, the more power others have. All perceived pain is of the ego and of the world the ego has made; the spirit is invulnerable.

The ego has made a world of separation, conflict, confusion, fear, anger, anguish, enemies, limitations, loss, and lack. For the ego to survive, it must seek and maintain separation, conflict, confusion, fear, anger, anguish, enemies, limitations, loss, and lack.

So, what is the potential pitfall of my philosophy?

The potential for a lack of loving-kindness is a very real possibility.

If I believe that I am totally responsible for the things that happen to me, that I have brought them to myself, and that I have chosen my reactions, then I believe that my fellow brothers and sisters in this experiment we call life have done the same. If that is so, then one could possibly conclude there is no need for compassion, caring, nurturing, helping, or even reaching out.

I could possibly take the position: everyone has chosen the events in their lives for themselves and their own spiritual edification, and so I will have no need for loving- kindness toward them; they can live their experience as they choose. Why should I interfere? Why should I care?

The position of no loving-kindness is the position of detachment instead of the loving non-attachment demonstrated in the Zen parable *Ah, so.*

I believe the way to the truth of our oneness is through nothing less than living loving-kindness toward each other every day. One of the greatest examples of loving- kindness I have ever heard came in an email forwarded to me from a friend. It has probably traveled around the world many times by now; I don't even know if it is true; I hope it is, and I want to share it here.

The email told of the story of a mother looking for her little boy, and when she went outside, she saw her son sitting on the lap of the elderly neighbor next door. Since she knew her son was safe, she went back inside and waited for him to come home. When he came through the door, she asked, out of habit, "Where he had been?" and he said, "Visiting Mr. Paul." "Oh," said the mother. Knowing that Mr. Paul had recently lost his wife, she asked, "What did you talk about?" "Nothing," said her son, matter-of-factly heading to his bedroom to play. "Then, what did you do while you were there?" asked the mother out of curiosity. "I helped him cry," her son said and walked on.

Wow! "I helped him cry." The little boy didn't try to fix anything or change anything; he was not sophisticated enough to determine whether Mr. Paul was a victim or not, or whether Mr. Paul had created his own circumstance; nor did he become mired in the depth of Mr. Paul's pain; he did not see Mr. Paul as a victim; he merely helped Mr. Paul live in his moment of grief; he provided the only comfort he knew how to give, he helped him cry and then came home.

I believe it is vital for us to stay connected, and I can do that best through loving- kindness. It is what we do when our teenagers go through their first heartbreak; often just providing a hug, no words of wisdom, no judgment, nothing but a secure, comforting hug, which says, "All will be well," and says, without utterance, "You are safe; you are spirit; you are love; you are invulnerable."

Loving-kindness is not the same as pity or sympathy; pity and sympathy confirm being a victim. Loving-kindness looks beyond the illusion of pain and sees the truth; it provides proof of truth by loving without having the need to change anything or anyone.

Unconditional love is the only thing in life that can make us feel truly safe; it is the only thing that everyone's soul knows is real and everlasting.

Unconditional love is the only thing that can heal us when
we realize we need healing.

#92 The Egret

I had never really understood it. *A Course in Miracles*, and many other pathways to spiritual truth, teaches that there is nothing outside of us: all is within. That's a hard concept to grasp when we are constantly bombarded with stimuli that seem to prove otherwise.

Then a rather strange moment allowed me a brief glimpse into our oneness and into the concept that all is within - nothing is without.

I parked in the carport, situated some distance from my condo, and started my relatively long walk to my home. I turned the corner and stopped abruptly in my tracks.

The sun was shining in my eyes. After blinking and squinting, I realized a beautiful, tall, long-necked egret stood at the intersection of sidewalks I needed to traverse to get to my door.

The egret was facing to my left, looking straight at me through the deep, dark, glistening eye on the side of his (?) head. I paused; I didn't want to scare it, but I wanted to continue walking forward, so I did the only thing I knew to do . . .

I explained to the egret, in a quiet gentle voice, "I live here."—I pointed politely to my place. I went on explaining, "My front door is a bit beyond you—over there." And I pointed around the corner to make sure he understood. "I'm sorry, but I'm going to have to pass by you to get home; I hope you don't mind."

He listened intently, stood statuesquely, and did not reply.

I moved to the far-left side of the walk and progressed slowly . . .

gently, keeping my eye on his eye the whole time.

To my surprise, he didn't fly away.

I resumed my one-sided conversation telling him how beautiful he was and how glad I was he had decided to visit this part of the neighborhood.

I got closer; he turned, and I expected him to take flight; instead, he gracefully strolled, with his long, slender legs to a grassy spot just beyond the juncture in the sidewalk where I needed to make another turn.

I now was within inches of him; I whispered, "I'm so glad I didn't frighten you. Thanks for trusting me." I smiled, made my turn, and headed toward the final bend onto a short walkway that leads up to my front door.

He hadn't budged. I started down the final stretch, glanced back, and saw him following me! He was now a foot or so behind, and he was *actually* following me.

I turned toward him, and cajoled, "My goodness, aren't you courageous! You are as brave as you are beautiful." I was standing inches from my front door when the egret started strolling down the short walk I was standing on; he was coming straight toward me as if he were going to go inside with me!

I maintained my "small talk," asking him what kind of day he was having and if he had a mate somewhere close by; he just watched.

Finally, I was ready to go in the house, so I said, "Well, thank you for such a wonderful encounter; I hope we meet again soon, but I have to go in now, so you have a wonderful day."

I turned, came in, shut the front door, and immediately positioned myself near the window so that I could see what the egret would do next but where he could not see me.

He waited, looking at the front door, for about five or six seconds, turned and sauntered down the sidewalk; he strutted as if he owned the place and had come to make an important inspection of the property and me.

. . . but little did I know what was to happen next!

I often walk down by the creek near my home, where ducks and egrets lounge. The day after "meeting" the egret, I went for a walk there and found myself seeking "my" egret—yes, I had made him "mine" now –we had connected, at least I felt we had.I had hoped to see him, but I didn't.

The next day, I took another walk, and again looked everywhere for my egret, when suddenly, I stopped in my tracks.

I did not stop because I saw him; in fact, the egret was nowhere to be seen; that is not what stopped me, nor is that what made me stand motionless in the middle of the path with tears running down my cheeks.

The tears were not of sorrow, but of awe. I found myself standing there in awe. Not in awe of what I could see with my eyes, but in awe of what I heard; in awe of what it meant; in awe of what I was experiencing; in awe of what I suddenly came to know.

I heard *My SOUL* saying to me - as though I were speaking to myself - and yet I KNEW it was not me, "I need not see the egret with my eyes, for—I AM the egret!"

The words echoed in my head as I stood there frozen in a moment of complete knowingness - an inexplicable experience of the awareness that—I Am the egret.

There is nothing outside myself to see with my physical eyes for I am one with all that is - I am all there is—this "I AM" is not the "I am" of the ego, but is the "I AM" of Spirit—the eternal, ever loving, ever present, ever knowing "I AM."

At that moment I understood—no—I experienced my oneness with all that is. With one simple phrase, I awakened once again—even more aware than ever before - to the truth of who I am—that nothing is outside of me—that I am the egret, and I AM all that "being the egret" means.

I still find myself looking for "my" egret, but I no longer need to see the egret to feel complete, for I know that all I need do is remember—I AM the egret.

Your Thoughts:

#93 Dandelion Seeds

One day, after reading one of the lessons in the workbook section of *A Course in Miracles*, I went for my usual walk around the creek to contemplate the daily message.

It was a glorious spring day; nature was celebrating, baby rabbits were nibbling grass near the sidewalk, birds were singing praises to the morning, and the creek was bubbling merrily over the rocks creating a miniature waterfall for the ducks to play in.

I was feeling blissful, peaceful, and invulnerable, even spiritually invincible. Suddenly, I envisioned a memory from my childhood of many fluffy dandelion seeds floating playfully through the air right toward me. In my mind, I saw them bumping up against me and then falling away. Some clung to my clothes for a moment, but a mere puff of air sent them back into the breeze.

I sensed how completely harmless they were; they didn't pierce me or take root. They simply gently tapped me and floated away.

I began to see all the "slings and arrows" of life in the same way. They seemed small and harmless, merely little dandelion seeds bumping into me without an impact and then drifting away on the winds of time.

I will always remember the magnificence of that feeling, that oneness with God, and that realization of my true, invulnerable essence. Now, whenever the inevitable "slings and arrows" of life come my way, I remember the vision of the dandelion seeds and find peace and strength and joy.

So, I wish for you that all your trials and tribulations on earth are seen by your soul's eye as merely little dandelion seeds floating by with no ability to harm you or to take root in your life. Luv ya!

Epilogue

What Message Will We Write Today?

Each event in our lives is a blank slate upon which we write our own message. No message we write is ever neutral, though the slate upon which we write it is. Each message we write is always one of love or fear, peace or war, unity, or separation. No reaction to any message is ever neutral—our response is always one of love or fear, peace or war, unity, or separation. *The everlasting beauty is - we get to choose.*

Your Thoughts:

Acknowledgments

This book is written with gratitude for the many writings, insights, experiences, and gifts of wisdom given to me by previous spiritual seekers who have helped to pave the way for my personal spiritual journey to the Sacred Chamber within.

Special thanks to Ralph Durbin; his extraordinary generosity in spirit and support is the foundation for the publishing of my first book and this one, and for being the magnificent friend that he is and has always been.

Special thanks to Doug Dolan for his consistently wonderful advice and steadfast support and to Mellissia Christensen for her fabulous proofreading skills, fantastic enthusiasm, and her steadfast determination to apply the concepts of the book.

I would also like to thank Barbara Oilar and Kathie Bradley for their great insights, suggestions, and encouragement throughout the process of writing this book, and their keen eyes.

And to Dr. Linda McNamar for her wonderful Foreword and example in life.

And, I want to thank Adrian Baxter, a fabulous consultant, who gave me all the support I needed each time I needed it.

And it goes without saying, without Laura, this book would not be.

About Laura and Me

Upon reflection, I discovered Laura and I do, and have done, many things that contribute to our love for each other, so we are not just surviving but are thriving.

Along with keeping our spiritual relationship healthy, honest communication has been the foundation of our relationship, especially during the most difficult of times. If I feel resentment, I tell Laura, and I let her know I needed her help to get past it.

My resentment is my responsibility, but in sharing why I feel resentful, without blaming her, we can both work on how the resentment can be resolved. If Laura feels something is unfair, she shares it, and we would work it out. We do not harbor negative feelings, and we never go to sleep without resolving any issues, no matter how late we needed to stay up.

"Luv ya" are always the last words we say to each other.

We maintain mutual respect for each other as individuals and as partners. If I take out the trash, Laura says, "Thank you." If Laura does the laundry, I say, "Thank you." We don't let a day go by without expressing appreciation for all the things each of us does for the other.

We don't work at our relationship, we invest in it every day, and we enjoy the rewards of that investment. We support each other's dreams. When Laura decided to go back to school, I did everything I could to help her. When I wanted my master's, Laura did everything to help me. When Laura wanted her master's, I helped her. When I wanted the Acting Studio, Laura was right there by my side. Neither of us would have accomplished the things we have without the genuine, joyful, mutual support we share.

We stay actively involved in each other's lives. I often provide free workshops for Laura's nurses on Effective Communication, Critical Thinking Skills, and Management seminars. Laura is always involved with the shows I am in or directing. We have lots to talk about and share and lots of ways to enhance the quality of each other's lives; that's our goal—to ensure the highest quality of each other's lives.

But I think the most important thing we have done is to have decided very early in our relationship that we would not do anything we could not honestly do with love. That goes for chores around the house and personal pleasures.

It's funny when I share this concept with friends; they tend to imagine dishes piled to the ceiling, dirty laundry everywhere, and dust an inch thick, so they are pleasantly surprised when they come over and find all is neat and clean and organized.

Doing only that which we can do with love - not having specific chores and responsibilities but working as a team - is what created the foundation for us to embrace each other's freedom to be who we are without layers and layers of "*shoulds*," "*musts*," and "*need tos*" piled on top of us. It is a wonderful way to live.

We do not resent when either of us does not want to do something. I love to have my back rubbed. If I ask Laura to rub my back, and she does not want to at that time, I do not feel resentful or think she does not love me. I genuinely honor her freedom. What is most important is that, if I ask her to rub my back, and she does, I know it is out of love, not obligation, and the back rub is wonderful. It is also very special when she asks me if I want a back rub without my even asking her.

Laura loves her feet tickled—yes, tickled—I will never understand that, honestly, and I will tickle her feet when I can do it with love, either when she asks or when I want to do it for her without her asking. There is something special when you know that what someone is doing for you is out of love and nothing more and nothing less.

By knowing this happy ending, the value of the events that got us here will not get lost in some of the seemingly "negative" life-changing events we have experienced.

Everything has worked together for our spiritual well-being.

Luv ya!

Your Thoughts:

Appendix A

A Summary of My Beliefs

1. We are unconditional love. We are freedom. We are peace. We are joy.

2. There is a spiritual entity, a single life force known by many different names.

3. The full essence of that spiritual entity is The Spirit of Unconditional Love.

4. Our true essence is the same—The Spirit of Unconditional Love.

5. We are one with God/Source and all that is real.

6. Our egos have temporarily blinded us to our *awareness* of our true essence.

7. Our purpose in life is to awaken fully to our oneness with THE SOUL, and with each other, by taking the following four steps:

   a. To discover (or rediscover or uncover)—unconditional love

   b. To come to understand unconditional love

   c. To come to live unconditional love

   d. To come to "be" our true essence: unconditional love.

This purpose can be, and will be, fulfilled by every soul!

Our spiritual journeys aren't linear or vertical, horizontal, or external, internal, or circular or spiral; our spiritual journeys do not move us in any direction; they simply unveil the truth of who we are: eternal threads of unconditional love woven together by God.

Appendix B

My Tenets of Faith

1. The Spirit of Unconditional Love (The SOUL) is known by many names including God, Source, Allah, Christ, Buddha, Jehovah, and many more.

2. We are one with each other and with The SOUL.

3. Unconditional love is: Thought that is without condemnation, founded on faith that is without doubt, fueled by emotion that is without fear, fused with kindness that is without boundary.

4. Unconditional love is understanding, patient, kind, gentle, humble, strong, hopeful, faithful, wise, compassionate, infinite, and eternal.

5. Unconditional love lifts people up and seeks only itself in all things

6. Unconditional love is free from attachments, condemnation, doubt, fear, needs, grievances, pain, vengefulness, and attack and creates everlasting peace and joy.

7. Everyone is always doing the best they can at that moment in their lives.

8. Each of us is a child of THE SOUL and is created spiritually in THE SOUL's image.

9. THE SOUL is the only source of life's energy.

10. People of all beliefs can discover, understand, live, and "be" unconditional love.

11. Any person who seeks THE SOUL will find THE SOUL.

12. Each of us will achieve awareness of his/her oneness with THE SOUL.

13. We all are always exactly where we need to be to achieve full enlightenment.

14. All things work together for our spiritual well-being as we seek THE SOUL.

15. The temporal world is an illusion in that it has no meaning other than what we give it.

16. Truth is not susceptible to interpretation; it never changes; it is eternal and infinite.

17. THE SOUL is in the "everywhere," the "every when" and embraces the "everyone."

18. Everyone is born with all spiritual knowledge and love.

19. Everyone can touch "god" directly—there is no separation.

20. The only thing each of us needs to do is to seek inward—seek to discover, understand, live, and "be" unconditional love in our everyday lives.

21. The pursuit of unconditional love can spring from any river of spirituality.

22. Unconditional love is boundless, eternal, infinite, and all-encompassing.

23. Unconditional love is free from doctrine.

24. We are invulnerable because we are spirit.

25. THE Spirit of Unconditional Love speaks to everyone; we need only listen.

26. Each event in our lives is a blank slate upon which we write our own message. No message we write is ever neutral, though the slate upon which we write it is. Each message we write is always one of love or fear, peace or war, unity or separation. No reaction to any message is ever neutral—our response is always one of love or fear, peace or war, unity or separation. The everlasting beauty is - we get to choose.

27. "Nothing real can be threatened. Nothing unreal exists. Herein lies the peace of God."[26]

28. Unconditional love embraces everyone's unfettered freedom and thus celebrates its own.

29. The key question to ask when reading any work of religious philosophy is, "Does this material help me create and solidify an indestructible bond of unconditional love with The SOUL and with *every* person on earth?" If the answer is yes, then it is spiritual truth. If the material you are reading suggests anything that would create a separation from God and/or a separation from any human being on earth, then the material is not spiritual truth.

References

1. Alvino, G. (1972, November 28). The human energy field in relation to science, consciousness, and health. *New York Post, Part 2.*
2. Frankl, Viktor E. (2,000). *Man's Search for Meaning* Retrieved from https://www.bing.com/search?q=https%3A%2F%2Fwww.goodreads.com%2Fauthor%2Fquotes%2F2782%0A&form=IPRV10#:~:text=https%3A//www.goodreads.com/author/quotes/2782.Viktor_E_Frankl%3Fpage%3D2
3. Reps, Paul (1989). *Zen Flesh, Zen Bones.* New York, NY: Doubleday Dell Publishing. "A Cup of Tea" (p. 5).
4. First people-The legends. (n.d.). Retrieved from http://www.firstpeople.us/FP- Html/Legends/TwoWolves-Cherokee.html
5. Reps, Paul (1989). *Zen Flesh, Zen Bones.* New York, NY: Doubleday Dell Publishing. "Muddy Road" (p. 18).
6. Keats, John. "Ode on a Grecian Urn" Retrieved from http://www.eecs.harvard.edu/~keith/poems/urn.html
7. Jong, E. (n.d.) Retrieved from: http://www.goodreads.com/author/quotes/6085 Jong, Erica
8. Think Exist.com, Swindoll, C.R. (n.d.) Retrieved from: http://thinkexist.com/quotation/we-are-all- faced-with-a-series-of- great/406608.html
9. Think Exist.com, Dewar, T. (n.d.) Retrieved from: http://thinkexist.com/quotation/minds_are_like_parachutes-they_work_best_when/213365.html
10. Edman, Irwin (1951). *Emerson's Essays.* New York, NY: Harper & Row, Publishers. "History" (p. 2).
11. Edman, Irwin (1951*). Emerson's Essays.* New York, NY: Harper & Row, Publishers. "History" (p. 17).
12. Edman, Irwin (1951). *Emerson's Essays.* New York, NY: Harper & Row, Publishers. "SELF- Reliance" (p. 35).
13. Edman, Irwin (1951). *Emerson's Essays.* New York, NY: Harper & Row, Publishers. "SELF- Reliance" (p. 41).
14. Edman, Irwin (1951). *Emerson's Essays.* New York, NY: Harper & Row, Publishers. "SELF- Reliance" (p. 66).
15. Edman, Irwin (1951). *Emerson's Essays.* New York, NY: Harper & Row, Publishers. "The OVER- SOUL" (p. 188).
16. Edman, Irwin (1951). *Emerson's Essays.* New York, NY: Harper & Row, Publishers. "OVER-SOUL" (p. 191).
17. Edman, Irwin (1951). *Emerson's Essays.* New York, NY: Harper & Row, Publishers. "OVER_SOUL" (p. 189).
18. Think Exist.com: Hillary, E. (n.d.) Retrieved from: http://thinkexist.

com/search/searchquotation.asp?search=It+is+not+the+mountain+we+-conquer+but+ ourselves.+%96+Edmund+Hillary.

19. Think Exist.com: Barrie, J.M. (n.d.) Retrieved from: http://en.thinkexist.com/search/searchQuotation.asp?search=Those+who+bring+sunshine+to+the+liv es+of+others+cannot+keep+it+from+themselves.%97+James+Brenthew+Barrie

20. Think Exist.com: James, W. (n.d.) Retrieved from: http://en.thinkexist.com/search/searchquotation.asp?search=The+greatest+discovery+of+any+generat ion+is+that+human+beings+-can+alter+their+lives+by+altering+their+attitudes.+%96+

21. Think Exist.com: Gibran K. (n.d.) Retrieved from: http://en.thinkexist.com/search/searchquotation.asp?search=Your+pain+is+the+breaking+of+the+shel l+that+encloses+your+understanding.+%96+Kahlil+Gibran

22. Active board. (n.d.). Retrieved from http://na.activeboard.com/t21471179/taoist-parable-who-knows- what-is-good-and-what-is-bad/

23. Staunton, Howard (1879). The Globe Illustrated Shakespeare, Avenel, NJ. Gramercy Books. "Hamlet" ACT II, SCENE ii (Hamlet, p. 1878).

24. Think Exist.com: Gibran, K. (n.d.) Retrieved from: http://thinkexist.com/search/searchquotation.asp?search=Say+not%2C+%93I+have+-found+the+truth%2C%94+but+rather%2C+I+have+-found+a+truth.%94+Say+not%2C+%93I+

25. Think Exist.com: Williams, B. (n.d.) Retrieved from: http://thinkexist.com/search/searchquotation.asp?search=If+we+try+and+-fail%2C+we+have+tempora ry+disappointment.+If+we+don%92t+try%2C+we+have+permanent+regret

26. Think Exist.com: Gibran, K. (n.d.) Retrieved from: http://thinkexist.com/search/searchquotation.asp?search=Of+the+good+in+you+I+can+-speak%2C+b ut+not+of+the+evil.+For+what+is+evil+but+good+tortured+by+its+own+hunger+and+thirst%3F+% 96+Kahlil+Gibran

27. Think Exist.com: Pritchard, M. (n.d.) Retrieved from: http://thinkexist.com/search/searchquotation.asp?search=Fear+is+the+dark-room+where+negatives+ar e+developed 123

28. Think Exist.com: Johnson, B. (n.d.) Retrieved from: http://books.google.com/books?id=F3fBXn2uoGsC&pg=PT84&d-q=A+brook+would+lose+its+song+if+God+removed+the+rocks+-+Barbara+Johnson

29. Staunton, Howard (1879). The Globe Illustrated Shakespeare, Avenel, NJ. Gramercy Books. "As You Like It" ACT II, SCENE vii (Jaques, p. 894,895).

30. Foundation for Inner Peace, (1992). *A Course in Miracles* (2nd ed.). Glen Ellen, CA: Foundation for Inner Peace, (p. 32).

31. Foundation for Inner Peace, (1992). *A course in miracles* (2nd ed.). Glen Ellen, CA: Foundation for Inner Peace, (p. 34).

32. Foundation for Inner Peace, (1992). *A course in miracles* (2nd ed.). Glen Ellen, CA: Foundation for Inner Peace, (p. 48).

33. Yogananda, Paramhansa. *Autobiography of a yogi*. Ananda sangha world-

wide. (n.d.). Retrieved from http://www.ananda.org/inspiration/books/
ay/ (30, The law of miracles p.261).

34. Yogananda, Paramhansa. *Autobiography of a yogi*. Ananda sangha world-
     wide. (n.d.). Retrieved from http://www.ananda.org/inspiration/books/
     ay/ (30, The law of miracles p.263).

35. Yogananda, Paramhansa. *Autobiography of a yogi*. Ananda sangha world-
     wide. (n.d.). Retrieved from http://www.ananda.org/inspiration/books/
     ay/ (30, The law of miracles p.263-264).

36. Yogananda, Paramhansa. *Autobiography of a yogi*. Ananda sangha world-
     wide. (n.d.). Retrieved from http://www.ananda.org/inspiration/books/
     ay/ (30, The law of miracles p.264).

37. AJ Consulting. (2005-2011). Retrieved from http://www.diamond-
     sutra.com/diamond sutratext/page1.html (3)

38. Foundation for Inner Peace, (1992). *A Course in Miracles* (2nd ed.).
     Glen Ellen, CA: Foundation for Inner Peace, (p. xiii).

39. Reps, Paul (1989). *Zen Flesh, Zen Bones*. New York, NY: Doubleday
     Dell Publishing. "Ah, So" (p. 7)

www.ingramcontent.com/pod-product-compliance
Lightning Source LLC
Chambersburg PA
CBHW030918120626
46554CB00001B/200